30 Bedtime Stories

FOR 30 VALUES FROM THE QURAN

COPYRIGHT © 2023 GOODHEARTED BOOKS INC.
info@goodheartedbooks.com

ISBN: 978-1-988779-65-2

Dépôt légal : bibliothèque et archives nationales du Québec, 2023.
Dépôt légal : bibliothèque et archives Canada, 2023.

Created by	: Bachar Karroum
Editor	: Tamara Rittershaus
Proofreader	: Christine Campbell
Graphic Designer	: Samuel Gabriel
Cover Designer	: Creative Hands

IN THE NAME OF ALLAH

30 Bedtime Stories For 30 Values from the Quran is a collection of 30 short stories that teach important life lessons and values inspired by the Quran. Designed for kids, these stories aim to promote personal development and growth through heartwarming tales that illustrate the value of kindness, compassion, honesty, patience, and other essential principles.

Each story is paired with a value from the Quran, making this book an excellent resource for parents and teachers to instill Islamic values in young minds. Join us on this journey of self-discovery and growth as we explore the wisdom of the Quran through engaging and meaningful stories.

GLOSSARY

♡ Allah	Arabic word for GOD
♡ Alhamdulillah	Thank God
♡ Assalam alaykum	Peace be upon you
♡ Bismillah	In the name of God
♡ DUA	Asking Allah for blessings upon yourself and others
♡ Iftar	Meal to break the fast during Ramadan
♡ InshaAllah	If God Wills
♡ Juz Amma	Part of the Quran, containing 30 chapters (surahs).
♡ MashaAllah	What God has willed
♡ PE	Physical Education
♡ Wa alaykum assalam	And upon you be peace

TABLE OF CONTENTS

BE POSITIVE

(216) (...) Perhaps you dislike something which is good for you and like something which is bad for you. Allah knows and you do not know.

Al-Baqarah (The Cow) 2.216

(...) وَعَسَىٰ أَنْ تَكْرَهُوا شَيْئًا وَهُوَ خَيْرٌ لَكُمْ ۖ وَعَسَىٰ أَنْ تُحِبُّوا شَيْئًا وَهُوَ شَرٌّ لَكُمْ ۗ وَاللَّهُ يَعْلَمُ وَأَنْتُمْ لَا تَعْلَمُونَ ﴿٢١٦﴾

STORY 1

TEAM TRYOUTS

Swish! When the soccer ball hit the net, Omar grabbed his sketchpad. He used quick pencil strokes to capture the force of the ball against the nylon threads.

"Omar, you're up!" Coach shouted, shaking Omar out of drawing mode.

Omar dropped his sketchpad on the sideline and ran onto the field.

"Three tries!" Coach said.

Omar's first shot was off to the left. His second shot was blocked by Hugo, who was trying out for goalkeeper. Omar's third shot went over Hugo's shoulder and into the corner. *Swish!*

"Yes!" Omar cheered.

After a few skill-practice sets, Omar ran back to the sideline to finish his drawing. He looked up every time he heard the *swish*. His friend, Phillip, had made two out of three shots. Hugo had made all three.

"Omar, you wanna try a turn as goalkeeper?" Coach asked.

"No, thanks," Omar said. He was sketching a pair of cleats swinging by its shoelaces. "I'm a midfielder all the way!"

After tryouts, Coach lined everyone up. "All right." He coughed. "Here's who made the team."

Omar clapped when Coach said his friends' names.

Coach listed thirteen boys then said, "The rest of you, better luck next year."

"Wait." Omar was stunned. "What? I didn't make the team? Not even as alternate?"

"I'm sorry, man," Coach said. "These other boys tried harder."

Omar raced home. He sketched a weeping willow tree, its branches drooping in heavy rain. A teardrop fell onto the page.

Omar's mother wiped his tears. "InshaAllah you'll make the team next year."

Omar huffed. "If I'm not on the team *this year*, I won't be good enough to play in middle school."

"You may dislike something that is good for you," his mother said, "but Allah knows things that you do not know. Time will tell."

***

At school on Monday, Omar's friends congratulated Phillip and Hugo for making the team.

"What happened, Omar?" a classmate asked.

Omar's face turned red. He wished he hadn't even tried out.

Omar walked home quickly after school every day. He couldn't stand to watch the other boys playing, wrestling, and joking on their way to soccer practice.

On Friday, as Omar walked home from school, the soccer team was heading to a pizza party. The boys in Hugo's mom's van were chanting team cheers. The boys in Coach's car were singing with the radio. Everyone was smiling, excited for their first game on Saturday.

Everyone except Omar.

He hurried home. He pulled out his sketchpad and drew a house, the roof being torn to shreds by a tornado. Then he crumpled up the drawing and threw it, knocking an envelope off his desk.

Dear Omar, the letter inside read,

> *You have demonstrated unique creativity and natural talent in your artwork. You*
> *are invited to join our elite Rising Artists Creative Club.*
> *The Rising Artists Creative Club creates together on weekdays at 3:00 PM.*
> *Please join us Saturday for our pizza social at Maple Lane Middle School to meet*
> *our members and our art teachers, and to learn about our community projects.*
> *We look forward to creating art with you!*

Omar was stunned. He looked at his cleats, his soccer ball, and at the dozens of pencil drawings laying around his room. He knew where he wanted to be, and it wasn't the soccer field.

"Alhamdulillah I'm not on the team!"

Sometimes things that don't seem fun at first can turn out to be good for us.
Even if we don't understand why something is happening, we should trust that
Allah knows what's best for us.

HONOR YOUR PARENTS

(23) Your Lord has commanded that you worship none but Him, and that you be good to your parents. If either of them or both of them reach old age with you, do not say to them a word of disrespect, nor scold them, but say to them kind words.

Al-Israa (The Night Journey) 17.23

وَقَضَىٰ رَبُّكَ أَلَّا تَعْبُدُوا إِلَّا إِيَّاهُ وَبِالْوَالِدَيْنِ إِحْسَانًا ۚ إِمَّا يَبْلُغَنَّ عِنْدَكَ الْكِبَرَ أَحَدُهُمَا أَوْ كِلَاهُمَا فَلَا تَقُلْ لَهُمَا أُفٍّ وَلَا تَنْهَرْهُمَا وَقُلْ لَهُمَا قَوْلًا كَرِيمًا ۝

STORY 2

GRANDMA'S GLASSES

"Assalam alaykum, Fatima. Get your library book and practice reading with me," Grandma said from her armchair.

"I don't want to!" Six-year-old Fatima crossed her arms. Ever since Grandma had moved in with Fatima's family, she had been bossing Fatima around. "You're not my mama."

Mama looked in from the kitchen. "Fatima! Please be polite to your grandma."

Fatima huffed and got out her book. She wiggled in next to Grandma. "*The little fox has red socks,*" she read. "*The* ... What's this word, Grandma?" Fatima pointed.

"Dear me, I can't see those tiny letters. Let me get my glasses." Grandma patted her head and her pockets. She checked the side table. "Oh dear, they're lost. Did I tell you I lost my glasses the night you were born?"

Fatima sighed. Grandma was always losing her glasses.

"Your mama called me from the hospital. I was so excited that I couldn't sleep, so I made a cake." Grandma raised her voice. "Zaynab, have you seen my glasses?"

Fatima's mother came to the door. "No, Mother, but I'll look."

"Oh well," Grandma said. "Fatima, keep reading."

"What about the cake?"

"What cake?" Grandma asked.

Fatima sighed. Grandma was always starting stories and getting distracted. "Never mind. What is G-I-R-A-F-F-E?"

"Giraffe," Grandma said with a nod.

"The giraffe has tall socks."

When Fatima finished her book, Mama came to Grandma. "Let me walk you to the table. It's time for lunch."

Grandma slowly stood, and they walked arm in arm.

***

After lunch, Fatima cleared away the dishes. "Here's Grandma's glasses! How did they end up in the sink?"

Mama laughed. She gently washed Grandma's glasses then handed them over.

"Oh, thank you, Zaynab. That reminds me, when you went to the hospital for Fatima's birth, I made a cake."

"You said that already!" Fatima interrupted.

Mama hugged Fatima and pulled her onto her lap. "Let's show Grandma respect and listen to her story."

When Fatima nodded, Grandma smiled. "Yes, yes, I put the cake in the oven, and I went to set the timer, but I couldn't see the tiny numbers. My glasses weren't on my head or in my pockets." Grandma patted her pockets again, pretending to search for her glasses. "They were lost."

Mama grinned and leaned closer to Grandma. "When you came to the hospital to meet Fatima, you *didn't* bring a cake! Did it *burn* without a timer?"

"Oh no, Zaynab." Grandma patted her daughter's arm. "It didn't burn—I watched the clock. When I took it out of the oven, something was poking out of the cake." Grandma's eyes lit up. "It was my glasses!"

Mama laughed. "Baked in the cake!"

Fatima giggled. "What did you do?"

"I had to dig my glasses out. The cake was inedible, so I had no choice but to throw it away."

Grandma, Mama, and Fatima laughed.

Mama hugged Grandma and gave her a kiss. "I love you, Mother."

"I love you, too, Zaynab." Grandma wiped a tear away. "And I love you, Fatima. I know I'm a lot of trouble, but I'm happy we can live together and *laugh* together."

Fatima liked laughing together. "I'm getting used to you living here," she said, "but I love you, and I'll try to be more respectful."

"Alhamdulillah for three generations of Muslim women!" Mama said. "Why don't we make a cake together?"

Fatima laughed. "As long as Grandma holds on to her glasses!"

Allah wants us to be nice and show respect to our parents. Even if we don't understand why they make certain rules, it's important to always be polite and kind to them. This is especially important as they get older.

BE OPEN-HEARTED

(8) But as for the one who came to you, eager 'to learn', (9) being in awe 'of Allah', (10) you were inattentive to him. (11) But no! This 'revelation' is truly a reminder. (12) So let whoever wills be mindful of it.

Abasa (He Frowned) 80.8-12

وَأَمَّا مَنْ جَاءَكَ يَسْعَىٰ ۝ وَهُوَ يَخْشَىٰ ۝ فَأَنْتَ عَنْهُ تَلَهَّىٰ ۝ كَلَّا إِنَّهَا تَذْكِرَةٌ ۝ فَمَنْ شَاءَ ذَكَرَهُ ۝

STORY 3

THE FORT

In Youssef's backyard, he and his neighbor, Mick, opened two large boxes.

"This will be the main part of the fort," Youssef said. "We'll connect this box to make a second room."

"Let's get started," Mick said, pulling scissors out of his backpack.

The boys cut an opening on each box and connected the two boxes with special two-sided tape. A second opening made the front doorway.

Mick folded the side of a third box. "Let's tape the roof in place. Ready, Youssef?"

"Assalam alaykum," came from a girl's voice. It was Youssef's younger cousin, Mariam. "You need a third person."

"Wa alaykum assalam," Youssef said. "Mariam, this is not your project."

"But she's right," Mick said. "The wind keeps blowing the box out of my hand. She could help."

Mariam took a corner of the box.

"No way," Youssef said. "If we let her help, she'll think she has all access to our fort."

Mariam backed away. The boys held the roof in place, and Youssef started taping it down.

Mick grimaced. "The wind is really pulling on it." His face was turning red.

"I'm hurrying," Youssef said. "Last piece of tape ... Finished!" Youssef flashed a smirk at Mariam.

Mariam was sorting through leftover boxes. "Let's build a tunnel. This box is long enough to connect the fort to the trampoline."

Mick's eyes lit up. "That's not a bad idea."

Youssef wrinkled his brow. "Forget it. No means no."

***

After lunch, the boys found Mariam stretching two long strands of twinkle lights over the fort.

"What are you doing?" Youssef asked. "This is *our* project!"

"Grandma gave me these lights," Mariam said. "Mick, can you help me make small holes to hold the lights in place?"

"Make your own holes," Youssef interrupted, "and don't get in our way." He went back to business. "Let's tape the door on one side so that it opens and closes."

As the boys worked, Mariam poked each tiny light through the cardboard roof. She taped a long box to make a narrow tunnel. Mick cut an opening and helped Mariam attach her tunnel.

"Who wants to go first?" Mariam asked.

Mick crouched under the trampoline and wiggled himself into the tunnel. He lay on his tummy and elbow-crawled through.

Mariam stretched the chord of the twinkle lights to an outlet on the porch. When she plugged in the lights, they sparkled on Mick's face.

Mick looked up and laughed. "It's like a starry night sky. Really cool, Mariam."

Youssef huffed. "The door would be really cool, if you helped me with it."

Mariam sat on the grass next to her cousin. "I know you wanted this to be a boys-only project, but Allah wants us to keep an open heart. It would be nice if you let me enjoy it."

Youssef sat silently.

Mick belly-crawled out of the narrow tunnel. "This is awesome!" He laughed until his eyes met Youssef's.

Youssef sighed. "It *is* awesome." He offered Mariam his hand. "Come on, cousin. InshaAllah I can fit through that narrow tunnel."

Allah wants us to keep our hearts open. We should always be kind to those who reach out to us, whether for friendship, help, or to learn.

BE GRATEFUL

(7) And 'remember' when your Lord proclaimed, 'If you are grateful, I will certainly give you more (...)'

Ibrahim (Ibrahim) 14.7

وَإِذْ تَأَذَّنَ رَبُّكُمْ لَئِنْ شَكَرْتُمْ لَأَزِيدَنَّكُمْ (...) ۝

STORY 4

ALHAMDULILLAH I HAVE YOU

"The baby will be here soon," Malak's mama rubbed her giant belly. "Yasmine's old room will be the baby's room, so you and Yasmine will share a bedroom."

"This baby is nothing but trouble." Six-year-old Malak wrinkled her brow. "I want my own room."

Mama pulled Malak close. "Let's be thankful that our family is growing."

"I have *nothing* to be thankful for," Malak huffed. "Our house is too small for another kid!"

Mama shook her head. "I'm grateful to have a house—a loving home for you, Yasmine, and the baby."

Mama and Malak helped Yasmine move her clothes and toys to her new room.

While Malak was doing her homework, Yasmine shrieked, "Malak, help me!"

Malak jumped. "What's wrong?"

"The hair ribbon came out!" Yasmine held up Becky, Malak's favorite doll. The doll's hair was a tangled mess.

"Give Becky to me!" Malak jerked the doll from her sister and tried to straighten its hair. "Her hair is ruined!" she shouted.

Yasmine's shoulders drooped. "I just wanted to brush her hair."

"That's *my* brush! *Ugh!* It's full of doll hair."

Mama rushed in. "Malak, why are you shouting?"

Malak clenched her fists. "She used my hairbrush. She ruined my doll. I can't do my homework. Yasmine shouldn't be in my room!"

"This is Yasmine's room, too," Mama said.

"I hate sharing my room!"

"Oh." Mama's face dropped. She held herself upright on Malak's dresser. She breathed slowly in and out. After a minute, she said, "Your baby brother is coming today InshaAllah! I need to call Aunt Khadija."

Mama rushed to make phone calls and pack her suitcase. Every few minutes, she stopped and held on to the furniture, breathing slowly. "InshaAllah Aunt Khadija will be here soon. Then Daddy can drive me to the hospital." She hugged her worried daughters. "Look, there's Aunt Khadija now."

When Mama was gone, Malak kept herself busy. She moved Becky and her other favorite toys to a higher shelf. She finished her homework and played by herself.

***

After dinner, Aunt Khadija came into the girls' room. "Your daddy just called. Your baby brother is here," she said. "Mama and baby are just fine."

"Alhamdulillah," Malak said.

Aunt Khadija wiped away happy tears. "Before they come home tomorrow, why don't we practice holding a real baby?" She picked up Becky from the shelf.

Malak sat with Aunt Khadija. She imagined holding her new brother. "I'm so thankful they're okay. Somehow, I love our baby, even though I haven't met him."

"When we are thankful, our love grows," Aunt Khadija said, laying the doll in Malak's arms.

"Rest the baby's head on your elbow to support his neck."

Yasmine climbed up on the bed. "I want to try!"

Malak showed her sister how to hold the baby. Yasmine giggled, pretending to cuddle and kiss her new brother.

"I know you'll be a good big sister," Malak said.

Yasmine smiled. "Just like you're *my* good big sister."

Malak blushed. She felt her love for Yasmine growing. "Alhamdulillah I have you, Yasmine."

"Alhamdulillah I have you, too, Malak." Yasmine held up Malak's hairbrush. "I cleaned out all the doll hair."

Malak smiled. "Can you help me fix Becky's hair?"

And together, they did.

Allah wants us to show gratitude for everything we have and to be grateful for the people in our lives. By being thankful, He gives us even more blessings. Let's always remember to thank Allah for all that we have.

GIVE FOR THE SAKE OF ALLAH

(264) O you who believe! Do not nullify your charitable deeds with reminders and hurtful words, like him who spends his wealth to be seen by the people, and does not believe in Allah and the Last Day (...)

Al-Baqarah (The Cow) 2.264

يَا أَيُّهَا الَّذِينَ آمَنُوا لَا تُبْطِلُوا صَدَقَاتِكُمْ بِالْمَنِّ وَالْأَذَى كَالَّذِي يُنْفِقُ مَالَهُ

رِئَاءَ النَّاسِ وَلَا يُؤْمِنُ بِاللَّهِ وَالْيَوْمِ الْآخِرِ (...) ۝

STORY 5

HAMZA'S APPLES

"I planted this tree for you when you were born." Hamza's mother pulled a branch down to eye level. "As you grow, the tree grows. Its apples are your apples."

The blooms had fallen off. Tiny green apples grew on the branches. Hamza checked them carefully.

"InshaAllah they will be delicious. I want to eat them all!"

Mama smiled. "InshaAllah there will be a lot more apples than last year."

Over the warm summer months, the apples grew and turned pinkish red. As school was starting in the fall, the apples were ripe. Every day, Hamza took an apple to school for his snack.

On the weekend, Hamza and Mama picked a bucket of apples and made an apple pie.

"Alhamdulillah for my delicious apples." Hamza ate his second slice of pie.

***

On Monday, he took an extra apple to school for his best friend, Ali.

"Thanks, Hamza," Ali said. "Your apples always look so yummy!"

The next day, he brought several extra apples. He shared them with the kids at his lunch table.

"This is the best apple I've ever had," Justin said between bites.

Henry nodded. "You're so lucky to have your own tree!"

Ali took a big bite. "Nom-nom!"

Walking home from school, Hamza tripped over a rotting apple on the ground. He showed it to his mom.

"What a waste," Mama said, throwing it into the trash.

"Mama, when I shared apples with my friends, I had a really good feeling. My heart was happy to see my friends happy. Let's give the apples away while they're still fresh."

"What a wonderful idea. Let's give them for the sake of Allah," Mama added.

Hamza wrinkled his brow. "For the sake of Allah?"

Mama smiled. "To give out of love for Allah, to someone in need and without expecting anything in return."

***

On Sunday, Ali came over to help Hamza. They picked apples until their arms were exhausted.

"MashaAllah, what a beautiful tree," Ali said.

Hamza sighed. "We're giving them away out of love for Allah."

The boys put the apples in two big boxes and loaded them into the car. Then everyone buckled up.

"Where to?" Mama asked.

"The children's home on 7th Avenue, please," Hamza said.

Hamza and Ali found the director of the children's home in her office.

"May we donate some homegrown apples?" he asked.

The director placed her hand on her heart. "That's so kind! Thank you." She pulled out a camera. "Let me take a picture of you with your donation so we can thank you in the newspaper!"

"Oh, no, thanks." Hamza shook his head, setting the heavy boxes down. "We just want to share our blessings."

The next week, Hamza's mother showed him the local newspaper. The headline read: *Fun with Apples at Pleasant Valley Home.*

> *A generous donation of fresh apples prompted a mini apple festival at Pleasant Valley Children's Home. After enjoying fresh apples and apple-themed games, the children and staff had fun making four apple pies and sixteen jars of applesauce. "We were blessed by this donation," Director SueMin Park said. "To continue blessing others, we shared eight jars of applesauce with the Wilshire Boulevard Homeless Shelter."*

Hamza recognized the director and several children from school in the photo. Everyone was grinning and holding a fresh apple. Hamza couldn't stop smiling.

Mama hugged him. "Your tree has slowly grown from a tiny sapling into a mature tree that honors us with fruit. You have grown from a tiny baby into a wise boy who honors Allah with his big heart."

When we help others, it's important to do it with a kind and honest heart. Giving just to show off is not true kindness. Let's always make sure our actions come from our love for Allah and helping others, without wanting praise or causing harm. Remember, true kindness comes from the heart and makes everyone happy and blessed.

EMBRACE DIVERSITY AND INCLUSION

(13) O humanity! Indeed, We created you from a male and a female, and made you into peoples and tribes so that you may 'get to' know one another. Surely the most noble of you in the sight of Allah is the most righteous among you (...)

Al-Hujurat (The Rooms) 49.13

يَا أَيُّهَا النَّاسُ إِنَّا خَلَقْنَاكُمْ مِنْ ذَكَرٍ وَأُنْثَىٰ وَجَعَلْنَاكُمْ شُعُوبًا وَقَبَائِلَ لِتَعَارَفُوا إِنَّ أَكْرَمَكُمْ عِنْدَ اللَّهِ أَتْقَاكُمْ (...) ﴿١٣﴾

STORY 6

MURAL DAY

"Tomorrow is Mural Day with my art club!" Omar couldn't stop smiling.

Hugo leaned in. "What are you painting?"

"InshaAllah the wall by the soccer fields."

"I know *where* you're painting!" Hugo said with a laugh. "What's the painting of?"

Omar's eyes lit up. "It's about the importance of bees. On the left, there are a few bees and a few flowers. On the right, tons of bees and tons of flowers. In the middle, a girl is walking into the sunset. It's going to be awesome!"

"It sounds really cool," Hugo said. "Good luck tomorrow."

***

At the city park the next day, Omar found his friend, Muhammad.

People who *weren't* from Maple Lane were unloading paint, ladders, tarps, and brushes.

Omar and Muhammad carried a tarp and unrolled it by the wall, bumping into another boy doing the same.

"Hey," Omar said. "Don't I know you? You played soccer for Otter Creek."

"I'm Alex," the boy said.

"I'm Omar with the Maple Lane Rising Artists Creative Club. You guys are in our space."

Alex crossed his arms. "Maple Lane is in Otter Creek's space."

Omar looked at Muhammad and his other friends. "But we're painting a mural here."

Alex stepped back. "No, Otter Creek Art Club is painting here."

"That can't be right," Omar said. "You guys have the wall facing the city pool."

"Nope." Alex shook his head. "This wall."

The Creative Club sponsor walked up. "Somehow, the city assigned the same wall to two different art clubs." He shook his head. "One group will have to move to the other side of the building."

Omar jumped forward. "Maple Lane works here. Our design has to be seen left to right."

Alex blurted out, "Otter Creek can't use the other side. There's a window right where two faces would be."

Muhammad spoke up, "Could we work together on this wall?"

Omar huffed. "No way these guys are talented enough to work with us. Plus, we don't want to work with people not from our community."

Alex shot back, "We're not working with Maple Lane!"

Omar crossed his arms. "We've been designing for months!"

"Our theme is too important," Alex said.

Everyone paused.

Omar cleared his throat. "What *is* your theme?"

"Embracing diversity," Alex said then smiled. "It has people of different cultures, religions, and abilities heading together into the sunset. It shows that we are all equal—everyone under the sun."

"Embracing diversity," Omar repeated. He thought about something his father would say. "*To set a good example—spreading positivity—I include others and embrace diversity.*"

"Our schools are rivals"—Omar unrolled a large parchment with their design—"but we both have good values."

"Oh, wow," Alex said. "Protecting the bees is so important." He then unrolled his club's design.

Omar and Alex overlaid the two designs and held them up to the sunlight.

Omar said. "If we make these bees a little smaller ..."

"And we move this boy's wheelchair to the left ..." Alex added.

"We can show the diverse group of people with the bees, combining the two themes!"

"Are you willing to work with kids from Otter Creek?" Alex asked.

They shook hands.

"It will be awesome!"

Together, they redesigned and started painting.

***

At lunchtime, Alex and Omar kicked around a soccer ball.

"It's been fun working together," Alex said.

"Yeah." Omar smiled. "Next year, we should design another mural for the wall by the city pool!"

In Allah's eyes, we are all equal, no matter our background, where we come from, or what we look like. What's important is how we treat others and live our lives in a good way. Let's try to be the best we can be, to be kind, respectful, and fair to others.

ALWAYS TELL THE TRUTH

(70) O believers! Be mindful of Allah, and say what is right. (71) He will bless your deeds for you, and forgive your sins. And whoever obeys Allah and His Messenger, has truly achieved a great triumph.

Al-Ahzab (The Combined Forces) 33.70-71

يَا أَيُّهَا الَّذِينَ آمَنُوا اتَّقُوا اللَّهَ وَقُولُوا قَوْلًا سَدِيدًا ۝ يُصْلِحْ لَكُمْ أَعْمَالَكُمْ وَيَغْفِرْ لَكُمْ ذُنُوبَكُمْ ۗ وَمَنْ يُطِعِ اللَّهَ وَرَسُولَهُ فَقَدْ فَازَ فَوْزًا عَظِيمًا ۝

STORY 7

THE SUMMER READING CHALLENGE

"Assalam alaykum, Hamza," Ali greeted his friend on the first day of first grade.

"Wa alaykum assalam," Hamza said. "What did you do over the summer?"

Ali shrugged. "Not much. I was mostly at home."

"Yeah, me, too." Hamza nodded. "But I read every book in the summer reading challenge, so InshaAllah I'm going to the pizza party!"

Ali bit his lip. "Oh yeah ... me, too." He shifted his eyes away from Hamza. "Hey, I'm going to stop by the library." He darted off.

"Okay, see you in class," Hamza said, but Ali was already out of sight.

Ali ran into the school library and grabbed the summer reading list. He wrote his name and checked off every book. There were twenty-four books on the list, but Ali hadn't really read *any* of them.

"Here's my list, Mrs. Monroe," Ali said.

"Oh, Ali, you read the whole list!" The librarian beamed. "Great job! Don't forget about the pizza party today at 11:30!"

"Thanks, Mrs. Monroe. See you then!" Ali said as he rushed to class.

***

At the pizza party, Mrs. Monroe announced, "Everyone here read *at least* twelve of the twenty-four books on the summer reading list! Congratulations! I've put your names in the hat. One of you will win this fancy new journal! Let's draw the winner."

"It's a cool journal."

"Pick me, Mrs. Monroe!"

"I hope I win!" echoed around the room.

"And the winner is ... Ali! Congratulations, Ali!"

Ali jumped. "Yay! Thank you! I never win anything!"

"Well, you deserve it! It's not easy to read so many books."

Ali blushed. He didn't dare tell Mrs. Monroe that he hadn't.

Mrs. Monroe pointed to the books. "Everyone, pick one book that you especially enjoyed to share with the group."

Ali found the thinnest one and flipped through the pictures. When it was his turn, he read the title, "*The Gruffalo*. It's about a little mouse and a monster, and they go on a fun adventure."

A girl raised her hand. "That's not what it's about! The gruffalo wants to eat the mouse, but the mouse plays a trick on him!"

"Oh." Ali shook his head. "Maybe I forgot."

Some girls giggled.

"It's okay," Mrs. Monroe said. "You can pick a book that you remember better."

All eyes were on Ali. He looked at the books that he hadn't read, at his classmates, and then down at his feet. His heart felt heavy. "I'm sorry. I didn't really read any of the books. I forgot about summer reading."

Gasp!

The room was silent until Hamza spoke up. "Why don't we start a book club? We can come to the library after school and read together. That way, we don't forget."

"We can have reading partners," a boy suggested.

"And share our favorite books," a girl said.

"I want to join," another said.

"Me, too."

"Me three!"

Hamza nudged Ali. "The library is full of great books. It's better if you read them rather than trick us."

"You're right," Ali said. "I shouldn't have lied. If I promise to tell the truth, can I join your club?"

"Of course," Hamza said.

Ali handed the journal back to Mrs. Monroe. "You should pick another winner. I don't deserve the prize."

Hamza interrupted, "Mrs. Monroe, can we *all* have the journal? We can use it for our club."

Mrs. Monroe smiled. "I think that's a great idea."

Hamza opened the journal to the first page. "Sign up *here* for the First-Grade Book Club!"

Allah likes when we are honest and never make up stories. Even if we make a mistake, lying about it won't help. It's better to be truthful so that others can trust us.

BE HUMBLE

(63) The servants of the Merciful are those who walk the earth in humility, and when the ignorant address them, they say, "Peace."

Al-Furqan (The Criterion) 25.63

وَعِبَادُ الرَّحْمَٰنِ الَّذِينَ يَمْشُونَ عَلَى الْأَرْضِ هَوْنًا وَإِذَا خَاطَبَهُمُ الْجَاهِلُونَ قَالُوا سَلَامًا ۝

STORY 8

FASTEST IN THE FIRST GRADE

"Assalam alaykum," Fatima greeted her friends at recess.

"Wa alaykum assalam," Malak said. "Do you want to play tag?"

Fatima jumped up. "I'm *it* first since I'm the fastest!"

"Three-second head start!" Jessica said.

Malak, Jessica, and Lily ran off. Fatima counted to three then raced across the schoolyard. Up the ladder, down the slide, around the play structure, back and forth.

"Got you!" she said, tagging Malak.

Malak quickly tagged Lily, who tagged Jessica, who tagged Malak again.

"I'll get you, Fatima!" Malak chased her.

After a while, Malak stopped to catch her breath. "You're just too fast!"

"I told you I'm the fastest," Fatima said. "I'm the fastest girl in the whole first grade!"

Lily clapped her hands. "Let's prove it." She shouted out on the playground, "Who wants to race Fatima for the fastest girl in first grade?"

Several first graders lined up.

Lily stood with her arms outstretched. "On your mark ..." she shouted. "Get set ... Go!"

Fatima raced and clapped Lily's hand. *Slap!*

The other racers followed. *Slap! Slap! Slap!*

Lily held Fatima's hand up. "We have a winner!"

Fatima cheered, "I'm the champion of the world!"

"You're the champion of *first grade*," Contessa, a second-grade girl, said. "You should race me."

Lily set up a new race. "On your mark … Get set … Go!"

Slap! Contessa clapped Lily's hand.

Slap! Slap! Slap! Fatima and the others followed.

Lily held up Contessa's hand. "We have a *new* champion of the world!"

Contessa cheered.

Still panting from the race, Fatima said, "I got second place!"

Contessa laughed meanly and moved closer to Fatima. "You lost. No first grader is as fast as me!"

"Whoa! We're just having fun," Fatima said.

"Race me again!" Contessa taunted. "I'll show you *twice* that I'm faster than you." She leaned closer to Fatima's face. "Or are you chicken?"

Fatima shook her head. "Please don't start a fight. You won the race. Now let's play something else."

"How about table tennis?" Malak suggested.

Contessa grabbed the ball. "I won the race. I serve first!"

Fatima shrugged. "Fair enough. I lost the race. I'll sit out. We can alternate when someone loses a point."

Contessa and Malak faced off against Lily and Jessica. Contessa served the ball to Lily, who hit it to Malak, who hit it to Jessica. Jessica missed the ball.

Contessa huffed. "You lost the point, Jessica. Rotate out!"

Jessica handed her paddle to Fatima. It was Fatima and Lily against Contessa and Malak.

After several rounds of girls alternating places, Fatima held the ball. "I can't believe you haven't rotated out yet," she said to Contessa.

Contessa crossed her arms. "I haven't lost a point," she said tensely. "I'm a table tennis champ!"

Fatima smiled. "You're really good. Can you teach me how you get that spin on the ball?"

"Oh." Contessa relaxed her stance. "Okay, yeah." She held the ball and a paddle. "So, you hit it here gently, across the top ..."

"Let me try!" Lily said.

"Me, too," Jessica said.

They took turns practicing. Soon, the girls were chatting, laughing, chasing after runaway balls, and encouraging one another.

Fatima held the ball. "We wouldn't have learned this trick if we'd spent recess bragging and proving who the fastest girl is." She served it to Contessa with a spin.

Allah wants us to be humble and avoid being arrogant. It's not good to show off and tell everyone how good or successful we are.

SHARE YOUR BLESSINGS

(215) They ask you what they should contribute. Say, "Whatever charity you give is for the parents, and the relatives, and the orphans, and the poor, and the traveler. Whatever good you do, Allah knows it."

Al-Baqarah (The Cow) 2.215 Revealed in Madinah

يَسْأَلُونَكَ مَاذَا يُنْفِقُونَ ۖ قُلْ مَا أَنْفَقْتُمْ مِنْ خَيْرٍ فَلِلْوَالِدَيْنِ وَالْأَقْرَبِينَ وَالْيَتَامَىٰ وَالْمَسَاكِينِ وَابْنِ السَّبِيلِ ۗ وَمَا تَفْعَلُوا مِنْ خَيْرٍ فَإِنَّ اللَّهَ بِهِ عَلِيمٌ ﴿٢١٥﴾

STORY 9

MARIAM'S BIKE

Mariam carried two big shopping bags. She rang the bell at her cousins' house.

Ding dong.

Eight-year-old Youssef peeked out before opening the door. "Assalam alaykum, Mariam."

"Wa alaykum assalam, Youssef. Is Sara here?"

"Yeah, let me get her." Youssef called to his five-year-old sister, "Saaaaaaara, Mariam is here."

Sara ran to the door. "Hi, Mariam."

Mariam showed Sara the bags. "Look what I brought for you!"

"*Eek!* Let's go through everything in my room," Sara said.

Piece by piece, Mariam pulled out her summer clothes from the previous year. "I loved wearing this shirt with the wildflowers. Oh, and look at this skirt."

Sara tried on the outfit. "I love it!" She went through the rest of the clothes, keeping everything her older cousin, Mariam, had to offer. "Thank you, Mariam. I really needed some summer clothes."

Youssef came to the door. "Hey Mariam, you know I got a bike for my birthday. My old bike is still too big for Sara. Dad said I could give it to you. Would you like it?"

Mariam jumped up. "The red bike? With the handle brakes? And all the gears? I'd love it!"

"Perfect. You can ride it home," Youssef said. "Maybe when you outgrow it, you can give it to Sara."

Mariam couldn't stop smiling. "Of course."

***

The next day at school, Mariam's first-grade class was at recess when Sara's kindergarten class walked by.

"Assalam alaykum, Mariam." Sara waved wildly. "Look, I've got my wildflower shirt on." She pointed to it and smiled.

Mariam ran over to high-five Sara. "You're wearing my old shirt!" she said loudly. "Don't I have good taste?" She looked around at Sara's class. "Sara wears all my old clothes."

Sara blushed. When her classmates giggled, her smile fell to a frown. She hurried off to class.

After school, Mariam was unlocking the red bike, the one with the handle breaks and all the gears, when a third-grade boy walked up.

He towered over Mariam. "Hey! What are you doing with Youssef's bike?" The boy crossed his arms and glared.

Youssef stepped between them. "Stop messing with my cousin. It's her bike. I used to ride it."

The boy looked confused. "Man, you were riding a girl's bike?" He laughed.

"It's a bike." Youssef stepped closer to the boy. "And it's Mariam's. So I guess it's a girl's bike. What does it matter?"

The third-grade boy stepped back. "Nothing, man. It's cool."

When the boy was out of earshot, Mariam said, "Thanks, Youssef. Why didn't you tell him I'm riding your bike?"

"It *was* my bike, but now it's yours," Youssef said. "Allah wants us to give and be generous, but not to make ourselves look good or to make the other person feel bad."

Mariam's heart sank. "I need to find Sara."

She ran through the school courtyard, looking for her little cousin.

Sara ducked to hide from Mariam, but it was too late.

Mariam knelt next to her. "I'm sorry I embarrassed you before," she whispered. "It's *your* shirt. And it looks lovely on *you*."

Sara smiled. The girls squeezed hands.

"Thanks," Sara said. "Do you want to walk home together?"

"Sure. Just let me get my bike."

Allah likes it when we share and don't waste things, and it's important to do so with humility. If we have an abundance of something, we should give some to our family or to those in need, without seeking recognition or praise.

FEED THE ONES IN NEED

(8) And they feed, for the love of Him, the poor, and the orphan, and the captive. (9) "We only feed you for the sake of Allah. We want from you neither compensation, nor gratitude."

Al-Insan (The Man) 76.8-9

وَيُطْعِمُونَ الطَّعَامَ عَلَىٰ حُبِّهِ مِسْكِينًا وَيَتِيمًا وَأَسِيرًا ۝ إِنَّمَا نُطْعِمُكُمْ لِوَجْهِ اللَّهِ لَا نُرِيدُ مِنْكُمْ جَزَاءً وَلَا شُكُورًا ۝

STORY 10

LEO

"Assalam alaykum, Mom."

"Wa alaykum assalam, Ahmad. How was school?"

"Fine, thanks." Ahmad set his lunchbox on the counter. "Can I have a sandwich? And an apple? Maybe some chips?"

Mom studied Ahmad. "You're awfully hungry. Did you eat your lunch at school?"

Ahmad opened his lunchbox. "Empty."

"You're growing," Mom said. "I'll get the turkey and cheese. You grab the bread."

Ahmad ate every bite. "Thanks, Mom. I'm going to do my homework."

Every day for a week, Ahmad had an empty lunchbox, but he was so hungry.

"Ahmad, I'm packing you big, healthy lunches for school. Are you throwing them away? Is someone stealing your food?"

Ahmad hung his head. "No, nothing like that."

Mom cleared her throat. "I sense that you are *not* eating your lunch at school. Please tell me the truth."

Ahmad met his mom's eyes. "I'm sorry." He wiped away a tear.

"For what, dear? What happened?"

"On Monday, on the way to school, a boy was playing at that abandoned house on 3rd Street, you know the one with the roof falling down and the broken windows?" Ahmad paused until Mom nodded. "He asked if I had any food, so I gave him half my sandwich. He ate it so fast. He must have been starving. I just gave him the rest of my lunch."

"That's very kind, Ahmad, but you also need to eat," Mom said.

"His name is Leo. He lives alone in that old house," Ahmad said, "but he smiles when he sees me. I like giving him my lunch."

"It gives our hearts joy to feed those in need, especially when we do it out of love for Allah and not to get anything in return," Ahmad's mother said. "What will Leo eat tomorrow—Saturday—when you don't bring him lunch?"

"I don't know," Ahmad said. "Maybe nothing."

"Then tomorrow, we'll take Leo some lunch InshaAllah," Mom said.

**

On Saturday morning, Ahmad and his mom took some healthy food over to 3rd Street.

"Leo?" Ahmad called.

A thin boy, about Ahmad's age, came outside, shaking his head. "No adults can know I live here! She'll call the police on me."

"I want to help," Ahmad's mother said. "I won't call the police."

Ahmad held out a bag. "We brought you some lunch."

Leo stepped closer and took the food. "Thanks," he said then ran inside the house.

On Sunday, they took Leo another lunch. Leo was more relaxed about Ahmad's mom being there.

"Where are your parents?" Mom asked.

"I don't know my dad," Leo said between bites of sandwich. "My mom said I was *trouble*, so she kicked me out."

Every school day, Ahmad's mother packed a lunch for Ahmad and a lunch for Leo. On the following Saturday, they went together to bring Leo some food. A car was parked in front of the old house.

Leo ran out, smiling. "I'm moving to Pleasant Valley Children's Home! They took me to visit this morning. Every kid has their own bed, and the adults take care of you. They even eat meals together, like a proper family." Leo held up a small trash bag. "I'm just getting my things."

"I'm happy for you, Leo," Ahmad said. "The kids from Pleasant Valley go to my school. Maybe I'll see you again soon?"

"I'd like that." Leo got in the car. "Thanks, Ahmad." He waved as they drove away.

Ahmad shrugged. "How did they know Leo lived here?"

"I *may* have called in a tip," his mother said.

"Mom! You said you wouldn't—"

"I did *not* call the police! I called the city and asked what services were available. Only when I knew they would help Leo did I tell them his name and where he was living."

"Alhamdulillah," Ahmad said. "And thanks, Mom, for helping me feed someone in need."

Allah wants us to help others who don't have enough. He gave us many blessings, including food. We should share what we have with others who need it. It's important to be kind and help others.

AVOID MAKING ASSUMPTIONS

(12) O you who have believed, avoid much [negative] assumption. Indeed, some assumption is sin. And do not spy or backbite each other (...)

Al-Hujurat (The Rooms) 49.12

يَا أَيُّهَا الَّذِينَ آمَنُوا اجْتَنِبُوا كَثِيرًا مِنَ الظَّنِّ إِنَّ بَعْضَ الظَّنِّ إِثْمٌ وَلَا تَجَسَّسُوا وَلَا يَغْتَبْ بَعْضُكُمْ بَعْضًا (...) ۝

STORY 11

YOU'RE A GOOD FRIEND, SAMIRA

Samira rushed with her lunch tray to sit with her friends. Lily and Jessica scooted over to make room on the bench.

"Why is Layla sitting over there?" Samira asked. "By herself?"

Lily laughed. "I guess she's too cool for us!"

"Layla!" Samira hollered. "Come sit with us!"

Layla shook her head then quickly looked down at her lunch.

Jessica whispered, "She's mad at us!"

"She is!" Samira said. "What did we do?"

Lily giggled. "Maybe *we* got too cool for *her!*"

***

At recess, Layla sat on a bench. Fatima joined Samira, Lily, and Jessica, playing tag. Everyone was talking about Layla.

"What's wrong with Layla?"

"She's mad at us."

"She doesn't want to be our friend!"

"She's too cool to play with us!"

Malak ran over. "Can I play, too?"

Jessica tapped Malak's shoulder. "You're *it!*"

Everyone ran away.

Malak tagged the one girl who didn't run away—Layla. "You're *it!*"

Layla didn't move. "I'm not playing," she said softly.

"But you always play ..."

Lily ran by, shouting, "She's too cool for us!"

"We're not friends with Layla anymore," Jessica said.

As Malak ran after the others, Samira shouted, "Enough! Time out. Everybody, come here."

The group gathered around Samira.

"Layla is our friend," Samira said. "We shouldn't talk about her like that."

Lily huffed. "She's been snubbing us all day."

Jessica nodded. "I don't like her attitude."

Samira shook her head. "Did anyone ask her why?"

Fatima challenged Samira, "She's your best friend. You should talk to her."

Just then, the bell rang. It was time for class.

Samira ran to catch up with Layla. "Layla, wait!"

Layla didn't slow down. "I need to get to class."

Samira quickened her step to walk with Layla. "You always sit with me and play with me. Are we still friends?"

Layla gave her a small smile. "Yes, we're still friends. Best friends."

"Are you mad at me?"

"No. I wanted to be alone."

Samira used a serious tone. "Is everything okay?"

"Yes." Layla slowed her step. "Well, no." She wiped away a tear. "My dad has cancer," Layla said, crying. "The doctors give him chemotherapy—strong medicine to kill the cancer—but the medicine makes Dad feel even sicker."

"I'm so sorry," Samira said, walking Layla to class.

"I'm worried about him," Layla said. "Yesterday, he didn't even get out of bed. He was weak and in pain."

Samira hugged Layla. "I'm sorry. I assumed you were snubbing us. Thanks for telling me about your dad. I will pray for him."

"Thank you. InshaAllah he will feel better today, and in a few months, the cancer will be gone."

***

The next day at lunch, Samira was about to sit with Lily when she stopped. "I'm going to talk with Layla."

Lily laughed. "Why? If she wanted to talk, she would sit *here* with us!"

"She's too cool for us," Jessica said between bites. "Remember?"

Samira shook her head. "She's going through something difficult at home. We should be supportive rather than making assumptions and talking behind her back." She walked across the lunchroom to Layla.

"How's your dad?" Samira asked as she walked up to her friend.

"A little better today, Alhamdulillah."

"Would you like to be alone?"

Layla shrugged. "I don't feel like chatting."

Samira set down her lunch tray. "I'm happy just to sit with you."

Layla half-smiled. "You're a good friend, Samira."

Allah tells us to avoid making assumptions. If we hear or think something negative about someone, we should pay attention and ask that person before assuming the worse.

CONTROL YOUR ANGER, AND FORGIVE

(134) 'They are' those who donate in prosperity and adversity, control their anger, and pardon others. And Allah loves the good-doers.

Ali 'Imran (Family of Imran) 3.134

الَّذِينَ يُنْفِقُونَ فِي السَّرَّاءِ وَالضَّرَّاءِ وَالْكَاظِمِينَ الْغَيْظَ وَالْعَافِينَ عَنِ النَّاسِ وَاللَّهُ يُحِبُّ الْمُحْسِنِينَ ۝

STORY 12

RAMI'S SUIT

Rami scooped sugar into his favorite mug and stirred before sipping his peppermint tea. "*Blech!* There was *salt* in the sugar bowl!" He made a sour face.

"I got you!" his brother, Ali, laughed loudly then mimicked Rami's look of disgust.

Rami shook his head. "*Yuck!* That was a lot of salt." But he couldn't help laughing a little.

Ali ran out the door. "Race you to the bus."

"I'm coming." Rami didn't race. He poured his tea out in the sink and left.

When Rami got to the street corner, Ali was crying. "Rami, the bus drove off! We missed it!"

For a moment, Rami panicked. *Can we get to school on time if we have to walk?*

"Wait a minute," he said. "Is this another joke?"

Ali laughed. "Tricked you! Your face was so funny!"

Rami sighed. "I'm getting tired of your jokes. Why not play a joke on someone else?"

"Because I loooooooove you," Ali said.

Rami laughed. "*This* is how you show love?" He playfully poked his little brother in the ribs. "Hey, don't forget we're leaving after school for Aunt Khadija's wedding."

Rami was excited for the wedding. Aunt Khadija had asked him to read a special passage for the wedding ceremony. Rami got a new suit and had practiced the reading so many times that he had it memorized.

***

They arrived early for the wedding so Rami could see where he would be for the reading, and then they went to greet their grandparents, aunts, uncles, and cousins. Everyone was dressed in their best and excited to see each other.

Rami shook hands with a cousin his same age. He used a formal tone as he repeated an expression he had heard on TV. "Adam, my man, you clean up well."

The boys laughed.

Adam pulled at his necktie. "I'm glad I don't have to wear a suit every day!"

"I feel so grown up," Rami said.

A waiter stopped next to them. "Would you care for a refreshing glass of juice?" he asked.

Everything felt so fancy.

"Yes, thank you." Rami reached for a glass.

Ali rushed up between Adam, Rami, and the waiter. "I'll get them for you!" Laughing, Ali grabbed two glasses.

The tray was suddenly unbalanced and tipped out of the waiter's hand, toppling a full glass of orange juice. As the glass crashed to the floor, orange juice splattered all over Rami's new suit.

Everyone gasped.

Rami blushed and let out a slow sigh. He didn't say a word.

Rami and Ali's dad rushed over. "Ali! How could you?"

Ali looked down. "I was just joking around."

Dad shook his head. "This was *not* a funny joke. The wedding starts in twenty minutes, and Rami has juice on his suit. You will have a consequence for—"

"Dad," Rami stopped him, "I need to borrow a suit!" He turned to Adam. "You live close by. Do you have something I could wear?"

"Uh ... Yeah. Maybe you can wear my suit from the school play?"

"Let's go!" Rami said.

Dad, Rami, and Adam rushed to Adam's house to change Rami's suit.

"It's a little tight," Rami said, looking in the mirror.

Adam took off his jacket. "Here, you wear my new suit, and I'll wear that one. I won't be in front of everyone like you will."

The boys switched jackets.

"Thanks, Adam. I sincerely appreciate it," Rami told him.

When they got back to the wedding, the doors were closed, and the music had begun.

"There are my nephews! Assalam alaykum." It was Aunt Khadija. She was dressed like a snow princess, waiting to enter the ceremony. "Rami, are you ready for the reading?"

"I am," Rami said.

"Great." Aunt Khadija turned to the wedding coordinator. "As soon as my nephews are seated, we can begin."

The wedding was beautiful, and everyone was happy for the new couple.

Rami stood before his family and read:

> *A Muslim wedding is a union of two hearts.*
> *Their bond of love is a symbol of faith, devotion, and trust.*
> *They promise to cherish each other, to forgive, and to support,*
> *through times of joy or times of hardship.*

> *May Allah bless this union with peace,*
> *And guide the couple as they walk side by side in this journey of life.*
> *The couple, with hands joined, vows to be true.*
> *May their love shine bright, like a brilliant flame.*

***

After the wedding, the boys sat at a big table with their families.

Ali spoke up, "Before we eat, I wanted to say that I'm sorry about the spilled juice. I was trying to be funny, but I almost made you late for the wedding."

"You *did* make me late for the wedding! Aunt Khadija had them wait for me," Rami said with a laugh.

Dad nodded. "Rami, when the juice hit you, I was stunned that you didn't react. Weren't you mad?"

"I was furious! But Allah loves it when we control our anger and forgive, so I stayed calm. My only thought was: how can I find a solution to this mess?"

"Are you still mad at your brother?" Dad asked.

"It wouldn't do any good to stay mad. I know Ali plays jokes on me because he loves me, so I forgive him."

"I *do* love you, brother!" Ali said. "And since you love my jokes, I'll keep thinking of new ones Inshallah!"

Rami laughed. "But please, not when I'm wearing a new suit!"

Allah loves when we can manage our anger and forgive others. It's okay to feel angry sometimes, but it's important to keep it under control. Let's try to stay calm and not hold a grudge against others.

DO NOT SPREAD GOSSIP

(10) And do not obey any vile swearer. (11) Backbiter, spreader of slander. (12) Preventer of good, transgressor, sinner.

Al-Qalam (The Pen) 68.10-12

وَلَا تُطِعْ كُلَّ حَلَّافٍ مَهِينٍ ۝ هَمَّازٍ مَشَّاءٍ بِنَمِيمٍ ۝
مَنَّاعٍ لِلْخَيْرِ مُعْتَدٍ أَثِيمٍ ۝

STORY 13

MUHAMMAD'S ART

Mr. Sanders was showing the Rising Artists Creative Club a new technique with watercolors. They painted designs with clear water then dropped paint into the design for a swirling effect.

Omar had written his name in cursive then filled the letters with green and blue drops of paint. The colors swirled, giving the letters green, blue, and turquoise stripes.

"I like it," Muhammad said. "Too bad my name is so long. The water would dry before I could add the colors." He laughed at the problem. "What do you think of mine?"

The whole class eyed Muhammad's work.

"MashaAllah!" their friend Rami said.

"That is awesome!" a girl said.

"Muhammad, that's really cool," Mr. Sanders added.

Muhammad had painted a city skyline at night with black and gray swirls. Above it was a blue and red crescent moon and a golden star. The blue and red swirled into purple in such a way that it looked like professional art.

"Thanks, everyone," Muhammad said, smiling. Then he sighed. "I have some bad news. After next week, I'm quitting Creative Club."

The room echoed with, "Noooo!"

"That's too bad!"

"But you're so good at art!"

Omar watched everyone's reaction to Muhammad. He had painted a spotlight, aimed at the form of a clown. He had added wild mixes of colors and used black ink to add a tiny ant, unnoticed by the clown on the stage.

Rami leaned over. "That's cool. Are you the clown or the ant?"

"It's just art," Omar answered.

"We should help Muhammad stay in Creative Club," Rami said.

"He doesn't *want* to stay," Omar replied. "He's done with Creative Club."

Rami shook his head. "But Muhammad is so creative."

"That's just it," Omar continued. "He already knows everything we learn here. It's not challenging for him."

"Maybe it's about the money," another boy said.

Omar scoffed. "Muhammad's dad has a good job. They can afford it. It's not *that* expensive."

Everyone was talking about Muhammad.

"He doesn't want to be here."

"He's leaving for another art club."

"We need his talent for the next Mural Day!"

"He's going to take art classes at the college."

"I'm going to talk to Muhammad myself," Rami said. "There's too much gossip going around."

Omar and a few other students followed Rami. They found Muhammad walking home.

"Muhammad," Rami called out. "Why don't you want to be in Creative Club?"

"I do want to!" Muhammad said.

"Then why are you leaving?"

Muhammad frowned. "We just don't have the money right now."

Omar laughed. "I doubt it! Your mom got a new car this summer."

Muhammad nodded. "We're selling the car. And maybe our house. My dad has some big medical bills, and we have to cut back on extras for a while."

When Omar saw a *"For Sale"* sign in Muhammad's yard, he hung his head in shame. "I'm sorry." He blushed. "I started a rumor that you don't want to be in Creative Club because I was jealous of your work."

"Don't be jealous!" Muhammad said. "I'm happy to teach you anything I know!"

"You're a good friend," Omar said, "and that's why InshaAllah we'll find a way for you to stay in Creative Club."

***

The next day, Omar had an announcement. "With Muhammad's permission, we've set up a fundraising campaign for his family. Please ask all your friends and family to donate." He handed out a flier with Muhammad's skyline painting and the website for the fundraiser.

Rami added, "I talked to the school office, and each afterschool program can offer one scholarship for a student to join for free. Mr. Sanders just has to fill out a form. Can we give Muhammad the Creative Club scholarship?"

"Yes!" the group said, and Mr. Sanders nodded.

"Great!" Omar said. "Now let's stop any gossip. A club works together. Let's make art!"

Allah does not like gossiping. It's important to be careful when spreading news or information you're not sure is true

ASSUME THE BEST IN OTHERS

(12) Why, when you heard about it, the believing men and women did not think well of one another, and say, "This is an obvious lie"?

An-Nur (The Light) 24.12

لَوْلَا إِذْ سَمِعْتُمُوهُ ظَنَّ الْمُؤْمِنُونَ وَالْمُؤْمِنَاتُ بِأَنْفُسِهِمْ خَيْرًا وَقَالُوا هَذَا إِفْكٌ مُبِينٌ ﴿١٢﴾

STORY 14

AHMAD'S PHONE

Early on Monday, Youssef and Mick were straining to look over Ahmad's shoulder at a small screen.

"You're so lucky!" Youssef said. "My parents won't let me get a phone until I'm twelve."

Ahmad smiled. "That's what my parents said, but my dad got a new phone and gave me his old one."

Mick nudged Ahmad in the ribs. "I bet you get it taken away before the end of the week."

Ahmad shrugged. "The teachers don't care if we use our phones *before* school."

A new boy ran over to the group. "Hey Ahmad, it's me, Leo!"

"Leo! Are you going to school here?"

"Yeah, it's my first day. I just met my teacher, Mrs. Matthews."

Ahmad stood up. "Guys, Youssef, Mick, this is Leo. We, um ... well, we met in my neighborhood, and we thought he might go to school here."

Leo smiled. "Here I am! I used to be homeless. I had to steal food to eat, but now I live at Pleasant Valley Children's Home, and I'm going to school with you guys."

Youssef stood to shake Leo's hand. "I'm in Mrs. Matthews' class with you."

The bell rang for school to start.

"Time to go!" Leo said.

Mick whispered to Ahmad, "He's a little too eager for school."

"He has a rough background," Ahmad said. "He's happy to be in a good place for once."

Youssef raised an eyebrow. "A *rough* background?"

Leo had overheard. "My mom was a bad example, so I made a lot of mistakes. But I'm trying to be good!"

"Mick and I are in Mrs. Gonzales' class," Ahmad said, "next door to Mrs. Matthews' class. We'll see you at recess."

Walking into class, Ahmad felt his pocket. "Oh no! My phone!"

Mick nodded toward Mrs. Gonzales. "She'll never let you go get it."

"I hope it's still there at recess," Ahmad said.

***

An hour later, when the recess bell rang, Ahmad finished tidying up the math materials then ran to the common area, looking for his phone. Leo was sitting where he'd last seen it.

"Leo, have you seen my phone? I had it here this morning."

"No, I didn't." Leo jumped up to look.

Youssef and Mick helped search, too.

When it became clear that it wasn't there, Youssef turned to Leo. "You took his phone, didn't you?"

"What? No!" Leo shook his head.

"You rushed out of class to get here before we did," Youssef said.

Mick gasped. "Leo used to steal to eat. He thinks he can just take what he wants."

Youssef moved closer to Leo. "You wanted a cell phone, and you took Ahmad's!"

"Stop!" Ahmad held up his hands. "Leo, did you take my phone?"

Leo clenched his fist. "I didn't take your stupid phone!" He stomped off.

"He took it," Youssef said.

"He's so guilty," Mick agreed.

"I don't know," Ahmad said. "Let's check in the office."

***

"Someone just turned this in," their principal said, holding up Ahmad's phone. "Is this yours?"

Ahmad reached for it. "Yes, thank you!"

The principal pulled back. "Ahmad, you know that playing on your phone is not allowed at school. I need a letter from your parents, giving you permission to have your phone back."

"Yes," Ahmad replied sadly, "I'll bring the letter tomorrow."

The boys slowly headed back to recess.

"We messed up," Youssef said.

"Don't feel bad," Ahmad told him. "My dad will want the phone back, so he'll write a letter. InshaAllah he won't be too mad."

"That's not why I feel bad," Youssef said. "It's Leo's first day, and we made assumptions about him that weren't true. He was so happy to be here, and I hate that we upset him."

"You're right," Ahmad said. "Allah wants us to seek the truth, not make assumptions."

Youssef ran ahead. "Leo, man, I'm sorry. We know you didn't take the phone."

Mick added, "We shouldn't have blamed you. It was really uncool of us."

Ahmad agreed. "Next time, we'll assume only the best."

Leo smiled. "Thanks, guys."

Always try to see the good in other people. If someone says bad things about someone else, or spreads rumors or lies, we should be careful not to believe them right away.

BE HOSPITABLE

(24) Has the story of Abraham's honorable guests reached you? (25) When they entered upon him, they said, "Peace." He said, "Peace, strangers." (26) Then he slipped away to his family, and brought a fatted calf. (27) He set it before them. He said, "Will you not eat?"

Adh-Dhariyat (The Winnowing Winds) 51.24-27

هَلْ أَتَاكَ حَدِيثُ ضَيْفِ إِبْرَاهِيمَ الْمُكْرَمِينَ ۝ إِذْ دَخَلُوا عَلَيْهِ فَقَالُوا سَلَامًا قَالَ سَلَامٌ قَوْمٌ مُنْكَرُونَ ۝ فَرَاغَ إِلَى أَهْلِهِ فَجَاءَ بِعِجْلٍ سَمِينٍ ۝ فَقَرَّبَهُ إِلَيْهِمْ قَالَ أَلَا تَأْكُلُونَ ۝

STORY 15

RAMADAN INVITATION

"Hey Hamza, why aren't you eating?" Lily sat next to her friend at the lunch table.

"I'm fasting today. Or, at least I'm trying to!" Hamza bemoaned.

Lily raised an eyebrow. "Fasting?"

"This is the holy month of Ramadan. Muslims from all around the world don't eat from sunrise to sunset. Kids can try fasting to prepare for when they're older."

"You go all day without eating?" Tim, sitting across the table from Hamza, asked with surprise.

"With God's help, we can do it," Hamza said.

"You must be starving by the end of the day," Lily commented.

"That's one of the reasons why we fast!" Hamza said, smiling. "To understand what it is like to be hungry."

"Interesting," Tim commented.

"But there are more reasons why we fast during Ramadan," Hamza continued.

"Can you tell us the other reasons?" Lily asked. "I always thought that Ramadan was about not eating during the day and eating like crazy in the evening."

"Why don't you come over and eat with us today? I'll tell you more about Ramadan. I promise!"

"That would be so cool. I'd love to!" Lily cheered.

"Me, too. I'm very curious," Tim said.

"Can I come, too?" Jessica, who was also sitting nearby, asked.

Excited, Hamza said, "This is going to be so much fun." Then he paused. *I shouldn't have invited my friends over without asking Mom first.*

Hamza was nervous for the rest of the afternoon. Would his mom be upset? Would they have enough food?

Hamza ran home after school. "Mom! I'm so sorry, but I accidentally invited my friends over without asking you."

Mom eyed Hamza. "You accidentally invited them over?"

"Well, I was just excited. They were interested in Ramadan, and I invited them to eat with us without thinking."

Mom lovingly put her arms over Hamza's shoulders. "Next time, you should ask me first, but I appreciate your friendly and welcoming attitude. You remind me of the Prophet Ibrahim (PBUH) and how he welcomed strangers into his home."

"And gave them food to eat!" Hamza added excitedly.

Mom nodded. "If more children are coming for iftar, then you can help me prepare the food."

"I'm happy to help," Hamza told her. "Can you text our address to Tim's, Lily's, and Jessica's parents?"

Without losing time, they started the baked chicken, the falafel, two salads, and a soup. Tim arrived early and helped set the table. When Lily arrived, she stirred the soup so Hamza's mom could check the chicken. When Jessica arrived, she joined everyone in the preparation.

With the great collaboration of everyone, the food was ready.

Everyone sat at the big dining table, waiting to eat.

"We can already feel the joy and the Ramadan spirit," Tim said.

"Do you hear that lovely voice?" Hamza asked. "It's the Adhan—the call to prayer. We can eat now."

After reciting the bismillah and the Iftar Dua, Mom and Dad invited everyone to start eating.

"As you can see, we have dates and glasses of water. We break our fast with them. They will provide us with quick energy and hydrate our bodies," Hamza explained.

After breaking the fast, everyone filled their plates. Hamza's friends were talking, laughing, and enjoying the taste of new foods.

Feeling joyful, Hamza said, "It's so fun to have you all here!"

"So, Hamza, you promised to tell us more about Ramadan," Tim said.

"You're right. Ramadan is a time to get closer to God, to be thankful for what we have, and to help those in need by doing good deeds and giving charity. And, as my parents always tell me, to keep those wonderful habits after Ramadan."

Mom and Dad watched Hamza, proud of their son.

"There is more to Ramadan," Hamza's father said with a smile. "But, at your age, you're good with this."

After they were finished eating, Hamza invited his friends to his room. He wanted to show them his daily routine during Ramadan.

"Here is my peaceful corner in the room. A place I created with the help of my parents. I use this prayer mat to pray every day." Hamza showed his friends how to pray and how many prostration times he should do during every prayer. "And here is my very precious book, the Quran. I read some verses every evening before going to sleep," Hamza added before lifting a notebook. "And finally, here is my logbook of the month. I use it to write all the good deeds, the charity I do, and the Dua and the Quran reading I do during the month."

Everyone was interested in the amazing things that could be done during Ramadan. They were impressed by all the good deeds and charity Hamza had done so far and what he was preparing to do for the following days. They felt grateful to have a good friend like Hamza.

***

It was the end of the day, and everyone was preparing to leave.

"I really appreciate my first experience of Ramadan. Thank you so much," Jessica said.

"I learned a lot about Ramadan," Tim added.

"Now I know it's not only about food," Lily said with a smile.

Everyone laughed.

Hamza grinned, feeling honoured to be a hospitable Muslim.

Allah wants us to be hospitable. When someone comes to visit, we should greet them warmly, offer them something to eat, and make sure they feel comfortable and at ease in our home.

BE RESPECTFUL, DO NOT MAKE FUN OF PEOPLE

(11) O believers! Do not let some 'men' ridicule others, they may be better than them, nor let 'some' women ridicule other women, they may be better than them. Do not defame one another, nor call each other by offensive nicknames (...)

Al-Hujurat (The Rooms) 49.11

يَا أَيُّهَا الَّذِينَ آمَنُوا لَا يَسْخَرْ قَوْمٌ مِنْ قَوْمٍ عَسَىٰ أَنْ يَكُونُوا خَيْرًا مِنْهُمْ وَلَا نِسَاءٌ مِنْ نِسَاءٍ عَسَىٰ أَنْ يَكُنَّ خَيْرًا مِنْهُنَّ ۖ وَلَا تَلْمِزُوا أَنْفُسَكُمْ وَلَا تَنَابَزُوا بِالْأَلْقَابِ (...) ﴿١١﴾

STORY 16

WENDY

"Assalam alaykum."

"Wa alaykum assalam." Samira set her backpack on the kitchen floor. "Guess what! A new girl, Wendy, is joining our class tomorrow. Mrs. Henderson says Wendy is *death!*"

"What?" Samira's mother asked in surprise.

"Yeah, she can't hear *anything*! She uses sign language to talk."

"Oh, Samira ..." Mom shook her head. "Wendy is not *death*; she's *deaf*. A deaf person doesn't have a sense of hearing."

"Oh." Samira nodded. "That makes more sense." She picked up her bag. "Can we go to the library to get a book about sign language? I want to tell her my name!"

"That's a lovely idea," Mom said, smiling.

***

The next day at recess, Samira practiced with her book. "Hello." A simple wave. "I'm"— touching her heart—"S-A-M-I-R-A." Oh, spelling her name with her fingers was a bit tricky.

She found Wendy and signed, "*Hello, I'm Samira.*"

Wendy flashed a huge smile and signed back, "*Hello, I'm Wendy ...*" but after that, Samira didn't understand.

Wendy signed to her interpreter, Mr. James.

Mr. James said, "Would you like to play hopscotch with me?"

"Um ... Okay," Samira said with uncertainty. "With you?"

"No, no," Mr. James said. "With Wendy. I'm just interpreting what she said."

Samira laughed. "This is confusing. I better learn sign language so I can talk to her myself!"

Wendy signed, and Mr. James interpreted, "Wendy would *love it* if you learned sign language!"

Jessica and Malak came over while Samira and Wendy played hopscotch.

"How come the new girl's dad follows her around school?" Jessica asked.

Samira looked confused. "Mr. James is your dad?" she asked.

Wendy shrugged and tapped her ear. She hadn't heard what they'd said.

Malak rolled her eyes. "What a baby! She can't answer a simple question!"

Samira said louder, "Is Mr. James your dad?"

Wendy watched Samira's lips then said out loud, "Not my dad! My interpreter."

Jessica and Malak giggled.

"Her voice is funny!" Jessica said. "She sounds like a duck!"

"Come on, Samira," Malak said, laughing. "Play with us instead of this dumb baby."

***

Later that morning, Mrs. Henderson had an announcement. "Hamza is sick today. We need a substitute to compete for Room 6 in the Math Olympics. Would anyone like to step in?"

Wendy raised her hand. "Me!"

"Thank you, Wendy," Mrs. Henderson said. "Room 6's team is now Tim, Malak, and Wendy."

Malak gasped then whispered, "Wendy is too slow for the Math Olympics! She talks like a baby!"

The whispers spread throughout the class.

"The deaf girl?"

"You're going to lose now!"

"She's a dummy."

After lunch, the whole first grade gathered in the auditorium. Tim, Malak, and Wendy sat at a table across from three children from Room 5. Mr. James stood next to their principal and interpreted the rules.

When the principal showed the first math problem, Wendy was the first to raise her hand. *"Forty-eight!"* she signed.

"Correct. Point to Room 6!"

Samira and her classmates from Room 6 cheered.

Question after question, Wendy knew the answers. The team from Room 5 got a few points for answering faster, but Room 6 never missed a point.

"I can't believe we won!" Jessica said.

"Alhamdulillah we're moving on to round two!" Samira said.

Round two was Room 6 against Room 4, and with Wendy's quick skills, Room 6 won again.

Wendy and Mr. James showed the kids from Room 6 how deaf people "clap" by waving their fingers in the air. "It doesn't make any sound, but it shows Wendy that you're cheering," Mr. James informed them.

Malak left the stage and ran to Samira. "Do you have your sign language book?"

Malak flipped through Samira's book and found the sign she was looking for. She asked Mr. James to interpret, "Wendy, you're so smart. You know math better than the rest of us. I shouldn't have made fun of you or called you a baby." Then, with her fist, she made a circle over her heart, signing, "I'm sorry."

Room 6 moved to the final round against Room 1. The whole class was excited, waving their fingers to cheer for Wendy as she led Room 6 to the win.

Allah wants us to be kind and say nice things to others. We shouldn't call people mean names or make fun of the way they look or talk. We should always be respectful and treat others the way we want to be treated.

ALWAYS DO GOOD

(34) Good and evil cannot be equal. Respond 'to evil' with what is best, then the one you are in a feud with will be like a close friend.

Fussilat (Explained in Detail) 41.34

وَلَا تَسْتَوِى الْحَسَنَةُ وَلَا السَّيِّئَةُ ادْفَعْ بِالَّتِى هِىَ أَحْسَنُ فَإِذَا الَّذِى بَيْنَكَ وَبَيْنَهُ عَدَاوَةٌ كَأَنَّهُ وَلِيٌّ حَمِيمٌ ۝

STORY 17

NO BULLIES IN ROOM 6

The day after the Math Olympics, Mrs. Henderson read *I Will Never Not Ever Eat a Tomato* to the first-grade class in Room 6. Everyone liked how, in the end of the story, the picky eater sneakily admits that tomatoes are her favorite.

Mrs. Henderson guided the class to write about trying something new. She hung the essays for everyone to read.

Hamza's read:

> *I didn't think I'd like avocado. It's green and slimy. My mom made a sandwich for me with cream cheese, avocado, and tomato and said I had to try a bite. It was yummy. Now I ask for avocado on every sandwich!*

Wendy's read:

> *I wanted to join the Math Olympics team, but I don't like to talk in front of people. To make it worse, some girls called me a dumb baby. I tried the Math Olympics, anyway, and I showed everyone that I'm good at math. My whole class cheered for me. One girl said sorry for making fun of me and calling me a dumb baby. I hope we can be friends.*

Reading the essay, Hamza gasped.

"What is it?" Ali asked.

"I can't believe this. Someone called Wendy a *dumb baby* on her first day of school." Hamza shook his head.

"It's because she's hard to talk to," Ali said.

"It doesn't matter. It's really bad to pick on someone or call them names, especially someone with a disability."

Ali shrugged. "It happens all the time. You and I have been picked on for being Muslim. My dad gets teased at work for his accent. My brother Rami was bullied for the color of his skin."

"It *shouldn't* happen, though," Hamza said. "We can all be brave and kind like Wendy and put a stop to bullying."

Ali jumped into a superhero pose and used a deep voice to say, *"Good will overcome evil!"*

"I want to show everyone how kindness wins over bullying. Will you help me make some posters?" Hamza asked.

Ali grabbed some big sheets of paper. Hamza got out the markers. As they drew, other kids joined.

Hamza and Ali made posters that read, *"Try being kind!" "Respect each other!"* and *"It's okay to be different!"*

Jessica and Lily made posters that read, *"Sit with someone new today!"* and *"Ask someone new to play!"*

Samira's read, *"Get to know me! Don't talk bad about me!"*

Wendy made a poster that read, *"Don't stop dreaming, even if someone picks on you!"*

By the end of their free period, the children in Room 6 had eight posters to hang around the school.

Mrs. Henderson spoke to the class, "You guys are creating a *positive school culture*. We want our class and our school to be a safe place where everyone feels special and included."

Hamza agreed. "We can *all* do better at not teasing or picking on other kids."

Ali jumped into his superhero pose and, in a deep voice, said, "*Together* we can stop all bullying!" He pointed to one of the new posters that read, "*No bullies in Room 6!*"

"That's right," Mrs. Henderson said. "You don't have to be best friends with everyone, but you can always be kind." She had the class take their seats. "And now it's time for math."

Ali raised his hand. "Can I partner with Wendy? She's very good at math!"

Hamza said, "Let's *all* sit with someone we've never worked with before."

Mrs. Henderson laughed. "Let's try it! Everyone switch seats."

Allah commands us to treat others with kindness and fairness, even in adversity. Respond to negativity with positivity and understanding, and you may find that even your enemies become your friends.

KEEP YOUR PROMISES

(2) O you who believe! Why do you say what you do not do?

(3) It is most hateful to Allah that you say what you do not do.

As-Saf (The Ranks) 61.2-3

يَا أَيُّهَا الَّذِينَ آمَنُوا لِمَ تَقُولُونَ مَا لَا تَفْعَلُونَ ۞ كَبُرَ مَقْتًا عِنْدَ اللَّهِ أَنْ تَقُولُوا مَا لَا تَفْعَلُونَ ۞

STORY 18

THE OBSTACLE COURSE

"We're having a competition," Coach Hall, the first-grade PE teacher, said. "Boys against girls!"

It was sports day for Room 6, and all the kids were excited to start the day in the gym.

Coach continued, "The winners will have a pizza party for lunch. The losers will have to pick up trash in the schoolyard."

Samira and Lily started a chant, "Girls! Girls! Girls!"

All the girls joined in.

The boys huddled up. The whispers flew.

"We've got to win."

"Work together."

"Beat the girls."

"Pizza! Pizza! Pizza!"

"I need everyone to make one promise," Coach Hall said, and everyone quieted. "You must play fair. If you can promise to play fair, we can have a great race!"

When everyone agreed, Coach Hall explained the obstacle course and how they would race in a relay from one side of the course to the other. "I recommend you put your strongest, fastest runner *last* to finish strong," he said.

Everyone lined up, and Coach Hall blew his whistle to start the race.

Off ran Jessica for the girls and Hamza for the boys. Side by side, they ran to the low balance beam and carefully walked across. They giant-stepped through rows of tires, went up a ladder, climbed across a rope bridge, ran down a ramp, and raced to tag the next person in line.

The next two, Layla and Tim, had to run the course backward, going up the ramp, across the rope bridge, down the ladder, through the tire obstacles, and across the low beam. They ran to tag Lily and Zander.

Every other girl and boy in the gym was cheering and screaming their friends' names.

By the fourth trip across the course, the boys were noticeably ahead of the girls. By the time the last runner for the boys, Ali, was tagged, the boys were way ahead.

"You can do this!" the girls encouraged Fatima, their fastest runner and the last girl in the relay. "Beat the boys! Think of the pizza party!"

Ali was already past the tires and grabbing the ladder as Fatima raced to close the gap. She dashed across the low beam and bounded through the tire obstacle.

"Go, Fatima, go!" the girls shouted.

Ali jumped onto the rope bridge when a rope suddenly snapped.

"Whoa!" His feet dropped, and he crashed to the ground. "*Ow!* My ankle!" he hollered.

Fatima was close by and ran to her friend. "Are you okay?"

Her teammates were screaming, "Go, Fatima, go! This is your chance! We can win this!"

"It hurts," Ali said, "but InshaAllah I can finish the race."

"You'll have to finish on the girls' course. The boys' bridge is out. Come on." Fatima helped him up, and they crossed to the girls' course. She helped Ali climb with one foot. Then, together, they crossed the rope bridge.

"Don't you want to win?" Ali asked as Fatima helped him down the ramp.

Fatima whispered, "If we finish together, we can share the pizza. Then both the girls and the boys can pick up trash. Besides, I promised to play fair, and it wouldn't be fair to race ahead just because your rope bridge broke."

Arm in arm, they crossed the finish line.

Allah wants us to always keep our promises and not break the trust that others have in us. We should always be honest and true to our word.

SPEND OR CONSUME WISELY

(67) And those who, when they spend, are neither wasteful nor stingy, but choose a middle course between that.

Al-Furqan (The Criterion) 25.67

وَالَّذِينَ إِذَا أَنْفَقُوا لَمْ يُسْرِفُوا وَلَمْ يَقْتُرُوا وَكَانَ بَيْنَ ذَلِكَ قَوَامًا ﴿٦٧﴾

STORY 19

THE BOOK FAIR

Layla and Samira spent their whole recess at the book fair. After lunch, they went again.

"I want all the books!" Samira cheered.

"Me, too!" Layla said. "Which one are you going to buy?"

"It's hard to decide. I have ten dollars, so I can get two of these books." Samira pointed to a series of chapter books with dragons and unicorns. "Or I could get *this!*" She held up a heavy book about world records.

Layla had an idea. "I have ten dollars, too! Together, we could get *four* books in the series. I'll read the first one then trade it with you. Then we can both read the whole series."

"Let's do it!" Samira said.

Mrs. Monroe, the librarian, shook her head. "Girls, you've taken too long to decide. It's time for class now. You can buy the books tomorrow."

"Aw ... man," Samira said, putting the books back on the shelf. "See you tomorrow, Mrs. Monroe."

The girls went to Mrs. Henderson's class for Language Arts then to the gym for PE. After school, they walked home together.

"I'm starving," Layla said. "Do you have anything left in your lunchbox?"

"No, sorry," Samira said. "I ate all I had."

"I'm always so hungry on PE days. Let's go get ice cream."

"I have to ask my mom first," Samira said.

When they got to her house, Samira's mom said no. "Why don't girls have a snack here? I'll make you a sandwich."

"No, thanks," Layla said. She then waved goodbye and hurried off to the ice cream shop.

***

At recess the next day, the girls rushed to the book fair to get their books. They lined up, each with two chapter books.

"Ten dollars," Mrs. Monroe said.

Layla counted out her money. "Oh no! I only have four dollars," she said.

"I'm sorry, Layla," Mrs. Monroe said. "You don't have enough money to buy any books."

"But Layla," Samira interrupted, "I thought you had ten dollars."

"I did," Layla answered, "but I spent six dollars at the ice cream shop yesterday. It's okay. You buy two books, and InshaAllah, I'll buy the other two next year."

Samira shrugged. "I don't want to start a series and wait a year to complete it. It was a good plan, but you didn't spend your money wisely. At this point, I'd rather just have the world records book."

They both put the chapter books back on the shelf.

Layla wiped away a tear. "I'm sorry."

"It's okay!" Samira hugged her friend. "None of this change the fact that you're my best friend."

"Thanks," Layla said.

Samira took Layla by the hand. "Come on; I'll buy you a book, and you pay me later."

Allah wants us to be mindful with our spending and utilization. We should avoid waste and excess, striking a balance in our fair usage.

BE KNOWLEDGEABLE

(114) Exalted is Allah, the True King! Do not rush to recite 'a revelation of' the Quran 'O Prophet' before it is 'properly' conveyed to you, and pray, "My Lord! Increase me in knowledge."

Taha (Ta-ha) 20.114

فَتَعَالَى اللَّهُ الْمَلِكُ الْحَقُّ ۗ وَلَا تَعْجَلْ بِالْقُرْآنِ مِنْ قَبْلِ أَنْ يُقْضَىٰ إِلَيْكَ وَحْيُهُ ۖ وَقُلْ رَبِّ زِدْنِي عِلْمًا ۝

STORY 20

AHMAD LEARNS ARABIC

"Three months with no soccer practice! What are we going to do with ourselves until the spring season?" Youssef asked Mick and Ahmad.

The third-grade boys' team had been practicing four days a week, plus games on Saturdays, so they would have free time during the winter months.

"My dad promised to tutor me in Arabic," Ahmad said. "He's really excited and has it all planned out like a real class."

"Why would you want to learn Arabic?" Mick asked. "Your dad should teach you French so you get all A's next year!"

Ahmad smiled. He felt lucky to have a multilingual family and looked forward to learning French in school. "When my family worships, we recite prayers in Arabic. I'd like to understand what we're saying."

Youssef shook his head. "You don't have to learn the whole language! Just memorize the words, like I do."

Ahmad grinned. "I've been going to the mosque since I was very little. I've already memorized all the Juz Amma surahs."

"Then you know enough," Youssef said with a shrug.

Ahmad shook his head. "I'm growing in my faith, so it's time to learn more."

"You take this too seriously," Mick said with a laugh. "No way I would use my free time learning an old language."

"The Quran is very old, but it's full of life. I learn so much from it. I'd like to read it for myself someday," Ahmad said.

***

Ahmad and his dad worked through a book to learn Arabic. After three months, Ahmad could read the beautiful letters and speak quite a bit of Arabic. Every time they practiced, Dad would smile and say, "I'm really proud of how much you've learned."

"It's still really hard to understand the Quran," Ahmad admitted.

"I know!" Dad said. "But these things take time. We'll keep studying the Quran together. Someday, you will read it for yourself."

***

At school the next day, Ahmad was distracted. It was almost time for the spring soccer season. *Is there a word for* soccer *in Arabic?* he thought during lunch break. He pulled out his phone, opened this Arabic-English Dictionary app, and typed in *"soccer."*

Mrs. Matthews cleared her throat. "Ahmad, you know phones aren't allowed at school."

"I'm sorry!" Ahmad quickly put the phone away. "I was looking up a word in the dictionary. I won't use my phone in school again. Please give me another chance."

"*Tsk, tsk, tsk*," Mrs. Matthews clicked her tongue. "Well, if it was to use the dictionary, I'll let it slide. Thank you for putting your phone away."

Youssef nudged Ahmad in the ribs. "Watch yourself, Ahmad," he said. "If you keep getting in trouble at school, you'll be in trouble with God. Allah's mercy runs out if you keep doing wrong."

Ahmad hung his head. *Is that true? Will Allah stop forgiving me if I make too many mistakes?* He thought about something he had read with his dad the day before.

After school, Ahmad showed Youssef a passage from the Quran on his phone.

لَا تَقْنَطُوا مِنْ رَحْمَةِ اللَّهِ

Ahmad read the letters, familiar sounds to them both. *"Don't lose hope in Allah's mercy,"* Ahmad translated. "It means we can always trust that Allah loves us and forgives us."

Youssef nodded. "That's a really comforting thought. I should learn some Arabic, too."

"And I should try harder not to get in trouble at school," Ahmad said. "I've got to run. Assalam alaykum."

He couldn't wait to tell his dad that he'd read the Quran for himself.

Allah wants us to always keep learning and growing our knowledge. It's essential never to stop learning, as it helps us become better people in our hearts and minds.

RETURN A GREETING IN A GOOD MANNER

(86) And when you are greeted, respond with a better greeting or at least similarly. Surely Allah is a vigilant Reckoner of all things.

An-Nisa (The Women) 4.86

وَإِذَا حُيِّيتُم بِتَحِيَّةٍ فَحَيُّوا بِأَحْسَنَ مِنْهَا أَوْ رُدُّوهَا ۗ إِنَّ اللَّهَ كَانَ عَلَىٰ كُلِّ شَيْءٍ حَسِيبًا ۝

STORY 21

GRANDPARENTS' DAY

The lunchroom was bursting with excitement. Everyone had invited their grandparents to lunch at school for Grandparents' Day.

Fatima held Grandma's hand. "Come, Grandma; I'll show you where my friends and I eat lunch."

When they got to the table, Tim was already there with his grandparents.

Tim's grandpa extended his hand. "Hello, I'm Kevin," he said. "This is my wife, Kathy."

Grandma shook their hands. "*Assalam alaykum*, Kevin. *Assalam alaykum*, Kathy. It's nice to meet you."

Fatima blushed. "Grandma!" she whispered. "You're embarrassing me. Just say *hello*." She opened her lunch and pulled out a sandwich for herself and a sandwich for Grandma.

Grandma settled into the seat beside her.

"What did your grandma say?" Tim asked.

"It's just a greeting in Arabic," Fatima said.

Grandma smiled warmly. "*Assalam alaykum* means *peace be upon you*. It's an ancient greeting that goes back to the Prophet Adam (PBUH), the first man, when he greeted the angels."

"Let's just use English, okay, Grandma?" Fatima interrupted her. "Look, there's our friend Jessica."

Jessica set her lunch tray on the table. "This is my *abuela*," she said, excitedly clapping her hands. "Her name is Flor. That means *flower* in Spanish!"

"Hello, Flor," Grandpa Kevin, Grandma Kathy, and all the kids said.

"*Assalam alaykum*, Flor," Grandma added.

Abuela Flor smiled and placed her hand over her heart. "*Mucho gusto.*"

Tim's eyes lit up. "What did your grandma say?"

"*Mucho gusto*," Jessica repeated. "It means *nice to meet* you in Spanish. You try. *Mu-cho gu-sto.*"

"*Mu-cho gu-sto*," Tim repeated.

"That's right," Jessica said. "Try it with my abuela!"

"*Mucho gusto*, Flor," Tim said, reaching out to shake her hand.

Abuela Flor had a big smile. "*Gracias*," she thanked Tim in Spanish.

"That's really cool," Fatima said. "I want to try! *Mu-cho gu-sto.*"

"You got it!" Jessica cheered.

Fatima had never used Spanish before. "This is fun! *Mucho gusto!*" she said to Abuela Flor.

As Jessica and her abuela sat down, Fatima whispered to Grandma, "Maybe my friends would like to learn to say *Assalam alaykum*."

"I'm sure they would," Grandma replied. "It's a nice feeling to return a greeting in a good manner."

Fatima shared her idea. "When Layla comes with her grandpa, let's greet him in Arabic!

Just say, *As-sa-lam A-lay-kom*."

Fatima's friends practiced, *"As-sa-lam A-lay-kom."*

"Hey guys," Layla greeted, setting her lunch on the table. "This is my grandpa, Muhammad."

"Assalam alaykum," the kids all said.

Grandpa Muhammad smiled. *"Wa alaykum assalam.* Peace be unto you, as well."

***

Surrounded by grandparents and friends, Fatima couldn't help but feel a sense of warmth and love. She was happy to share her culture and learn from others.

When the lunch period came to an end and the grandparents started to leave, Fatima hugged her grandma tightly and said, "I'm so glad you came today, Grandma. I'm proud of who I am because of you."

Grandma hugged her back. "I'm proud of you, too, my dear. Remember, always return a greeting with even more kindness and love."

Being polite is important to Allah. It's like showing love. When someone greets us, not only should we return the greeting but it's also better if we return the greeting nicely.

ALWAYS STAND FOR JUSTICE

(135) O you who believe! Stand firmly for justice, as witnesses to Allah, even if against yourselves, or your parents, or your relatives. Whether one is rich or poor, Allah takes care of both (...)

An-Nisa (The Women) 4.135

يَا أَيُّهَا الَّذِينَ آمَنُوا كُونُوا قَوَّامِينَ بِالْقِسْطِ شُهَدَاءَ لِلَّهِ وَلَوْ عَلَىٰ أَنْفُسِكُمْ أَوِ الْوَالِدَيْنِ وَالْأَقْرَبِينَ ۚ إِنْ يَكُنْ غَنِيًّا أَوْ فَقِيرًا فَاللَّهُ أَوْلَىٰ بِهِمَا (...) ۝

STORY 22

WATER BALLOONS

"Adam!" Ali hugged his older cousin. "Assalam alaykum!"

"Wa alaykum assalam," Adam returned. "I haven't seen you since Aunt Khadija's wedding!"

Ali's brother, Rami, offered a fist-bump. "Adam! How are you, man?"

"I'm good. Thanks for inviting me. I brought water balloons. We should have a water balloon fight tomorrow!"

"Tomorrow?" Rami asked. "Let's do it now!"

"Okay," Adam said, laughing. "Let me set my bag down, and I'll get them out."

When Rami took Adam to his room to dig the water balloons out of Adam's bag, Ali tagged along. But when the older boys went to the bathroom to fill the water balloons, it was too crowded for the three of them.

"Ali, can you give us some space?" Rami asked his little brother.

Ali stuck a handful of empty balloons into his pocket and wandered off to the kitchen. From behind the door, he spied on his brother and cousin. As soon as Rami and Adam went outside, Ali snuck back into the bathroom to fill his own stash of water balloons.

Ali could hear the older boys playing in the backyard. He hurriedly tied the last balloon. With the balloons in his shirt, he snuck out the front door and tiptoed around to the bushes so he could ambush Rami and Adam.

"Boys!" Mom yelled, interrupting Ali's plan. "Inside." She looked angry. "Noooow!"

Rami and Adam gave each other confused glances as they went inside the house.

Ali hid his stash of balloons, raced around the house, and snuck inside just in time to hear Mom say, "You left the faucet on in the bathroom! Look at this mess."

Water was dripping from the bathroom counter to the floor. Mom had stopped the spread of water with a towel, but there was a big mess.

"Oh no!" Adam said. "I'm so sorry, Aunt Salma."

"We will clean it up," Rami added.

Ali watched, wide-eyed. *I must have left the faucet on in my hurry*, he thought. *As long as my stash of balloons stays hidden, no one will know it was me.* He giggled.

"What's so funny?" Rami asked, coming back with a stack of towels.

"Oh, nothing," Ali replied.

"Adam, give me the rug," Rami said. "I'll hang it outside to dry."

Adam passed the rug over the puddle. "How could we have left the water on?"

"I'm sorry, man," Rami said. "This isn't how I imagined our sleepover—cleaning up a big mess."

"Yeah, I won't ever do *this* again," Adam said.

Ali blurted out, "Well, you should have let me fill water balloons with you!"

The boys looked at Ali, confused.

"Um, what?" Adam asked.

"It was me. I left the faucet on. Please don't say you won't do any more sleepovers!"

Adam laughed. "I meant that I won't ever flood the bathroom again! You're my favorite cousins; of course we'll have more sleepovers InshaAllah!"

"I'm sorry," Ali said. "It's only fair that I clean up."

"Get a towel." Rami pointed. "We can help you."

Ali jumped in to clean.

When the floor was dry, Rami said, "We've done our part. You can clean the countertop. Come on, Adam."

Ali finished up and put the wet towels in the washing machine. He knew that fessing up and facing the consequences had been the right thing to do.

He went outside to look for his brother and cousin.

Adam and Rami jumped out of the bushes. *"Ambush!"*

Splash! Splash! Splash! Splash! They hit Ali every time.

"We found a stash of balloons in the bushes," Adam said with a wink. "I wonder where they came from."

Ali picked up a balloon that hadn't burst. He laughed and threw it at his cousin.

Allah wants us to be just and truthful. We should always stand by the truth, apologize when we make mistakes, and make sure everything is fair. Allah likes it when we do what is right, even if it's hard.

APPRECIATE EVERY CONTRIBUTION, NO MATTER HOW SMALL

(79) Those who criticize the believers who give charity voluntarily, and ridicule those who find nothing to give except their own efforts—Allah ridicules them (...)

At-Tawbah (The Repentance) 9.79

الَّذِينَ يَلْمِزُونَ الْمُطَّوِّعِينَ مِنَ الْمُؤْمِنِينَ فِي الصَّدَقَاتِ وَالَّذِينَ لَا يَجِدُونَ إِلَّا

جُهْدَهُمْ فَيَسْخَرُونَ مِنْهُمْ ۙ سَخِرَ اللَّهُ مِنْهُمْ (...) ﴿٧٩﴾

STORY 23

YASMINE'S GIFT

"Malak," Mama said, "remember how last Ramadan, we picked out some clothes and toys to give to charity?"

Malak nodded. "And we drove to the children's hospital with a big box of baby clothes and books!"

"Exactly," Mama said. "This year, Yasmine is almost four years old, so she can learn about helping those in need, too. I want you to help her pick out some things to give away."

"Okay." Malak straightened her back and smiled proudly. "Come on, Yasmine. Let's go to our room."

Malak led Yasmine to her toy shelf. "Are there any toys that are still nice, but you don't play with anymore?"

Yasmine looked up and down. She wandered over to Malak's toy shelf and reached for Malak's favorite doll. "I can give away Becky."

"No, no, no. Becky is *my* doll. And I *don't* want to give her away!" Malak took Becky from her sister and placed the doll high on the shelf.

"What about this?" Yasmine picked up Malak's table tennis paddle.

"No. That's also mine. I use it at school," Malak said. "Look for something that's *yours*." Malak opened the closet doors and showed Yasmine some shirts and dresses. "Do these still fit?"

"Yes."

"All of them?" Malak asked.

"Yes," Yasmine answered.

Malak sighed. She started going through her own clothes, pulling out shirts and pants that were too small. She made a pile of donations on the bed. Then she added a few small dolls, a hat she had never worn, and the beautiful dress she had worn to her aunt's wedding.

"No!" Yasmine shouted. "You can't give that dress away! I want to keep it." She yanked it from the donations pile.

"It's *my* dress. I can give it away," Malak said, taking the dress back.

"Then give it to *meeeee!*" Yasmine cried. "I want to use it to play princesses." She reached for the dress again.

Malak sighed again. "Okay, I guess." She handed it to her sister. "But you're getting more things than you're giving away."

Yasmine put the dress in her costume box then pulled a wooden puzzle from the shelf. "I used to like this puzzle, but I don't play it anymore," she said, placing it on the pile of donations.

"Just one thing?" Malak asked, sounding irritated as she added two stuffed bears to the pile. "Can't you give more?"

Mama came into the room in time to hear Yasmine cry, "I don't want to give anything else!"

"Mama!" Malak pointed. "Yasmine only wants to give away one puzzle."

Mama sat on the bed and pulled her daughters into a hug. "It's okay, girls. Really. Malak, you are big and are giving away big things. Yasmine is small. She is learning what it means to give for the sake of Allah."

Malak nodded. "You're right. A nice puzzle can make a child happy. It's a good gift."

Yasmine gave her big sister a kiss on the cheek. "Next year, I'll give away the princess dress."

"InshaAllah," Malak said, hugging her.

Even the smallest contribution has value for Allah. We should never criticize those who contribute small amounts to charity or make small efforts. Allah does not approve of mocking people who are trying to do good.

VALIDATE THE TRUTH, DON'T ACCUSE WITHOUT EVIDENCE

(6) O you who believe! If a troublemaker brings you any news, investigate, lest you harm people out of ignorance, and you become regretful for what you have done.

Al-Hujurat (The Rooms) 49.6

يَا أَيُّهَا الَّذِينَ آمَنُوا إِنْ جَاءَكُمْ فَاسِقٌ بِنَبَإٍ فَتَبَيَّنُوا أَنْ تُصِيبُوا قَوْمًا بِجَهَالَةٍ فَتُصْبِحُوا عَلَىٰ مَا فَعَلْتُمْ نَادِمِينَ ﴿٦﴾

STORY 24

THE BROKEN SOUNDBOARD

Coach Hall was making an announcement over the loudspeaker. "All fourth-grade boys who played basketball during recess, please come to the gym for a short meeting."

"That doesn't sound good," Muhammad mumbled, looking at Phillip.

As they walked out of class, Phillip said, "I wonder what we did."

In the hallway, Muhammad and Phillip met Omar, Hugo, and some of the other boys who had played with them, all heading toward the gym.

"Are we in trouble?" Hugo asked.

"I don't know," Omar said. "Maybe he needs our help setting up for the Thanksgiving party."

The boys sighed in relief.

"I'm sure that's it. We didn't do anything wrong during recess," Hugo said.

The gym was decorated in fall colors with papier mâché turkeys strung in a line in front of the bleachers. Coach Hall was setting up the stereo and speakers, getting ready for the party.

"There you are," Coach Hall said. The boys could tell from his expression that they *were* in trouble. "I asked you not to play ball near the sound equipment, and now there's a knob broken on the soundboard. This is a very expensive piece of equipment. I want to know who did it."

The boys looked at each other, shocked.

"Coach," Muhammad started, "we played on the other court. Not here by the sound equipment."

Coach Hall nodded. "It certainly looks like a basketball hit the soundboard. Did you see any other students playing over here?"

"It must have been Omar," Phillip said. "He came over here."

Omar shook his head. "I ... I just walked by to see the party decorations."

Muhammad pointed. "You had a basketball with you."

"I ... I had a basketball, but I carried it. I didn't break any sound equipment."

Hugo snickered. "Are you sure? You're pretty clumsy with the ball!"

The boys laughed.

"It was definitely Omar," Phillip said.

Omar turned red. "I didn't do it. I promise." He turned away from his friends and wiped at a tear.

"Look at him. He's guilty!" a boy said.

"He's lying so he doesn't have to pay for the soundboard!" another said.

Muhammad stepped forward and spoke firmly, "Hey, that's enough. We don't have evidence to prove Omar did it."

The gym doors swung wide open. Some staff members were bringing in a bouncy castle for the party. A gust of wind from the open door caused the hanging turkey decorations to sway. One fell—*Crash!*—barely missing Muhammad and the sound equipment.

Muhammad picked it up. "Ah-ha!" Then he lay down on the gym floor and peeked under the bleachers. He reached under and pulled out a second papier mâché turkey, broken from its fall.

Hugo took it from Muhammad and held it up. "The turkey must have fallen on the soundboard. It's about as heavy as a basketball."

Muhammad stood up. "It must have landed there." He pointed to the soundboard, right at the broken knob. "And rolled under the bleachers."

Coach Hall took the turkey. "You must be right."

Omar sighed. "Alhamdulillah," he whispered.

Everyone turned toward him.

"I'm sorry I accused you," Muhammad said, putting a hand on Omar's shoulder.

The boys echoed, "Me, too."

"Sorry, man."

"We shouldn't have laughed at you."

"All right," Coach Hall said. "I need your help. Let's move the sound equipment out from under these decorations!"

And the boys got busy helping.

Before believing and spreading any news, make sure to check if it's true. Investigating first helps to prevent spreading false information and causing harm to others. This way, you can avoid making mistakes that you might feel sorry for later.

RESPECT THE BELONGINGS OF OTHERS

(29) O you who believe! Do not consume each other's wealth illicitly, but trade by mutual consent. And do not kill yourselves, for Allah is Merciful towards you.

An-Nisa (The Women) 4.29

يَا أَيُّهَا الَّذِينَ آمَنُوا لَا تَأْكُلُوا أَمْوَالَكُمْ بَيْنَكُمْ بِالْبَاطِلِ إِلَّا أَنْ تَكُونَ تِجَارَةً عَنْ تَرَاضٍ مِنْكُمْ ۚ وَلَا تَقْتُلُوا أَنْفُسَكُمْ ۚ إِنَّ اللَّهَ كَانَ بِكُمْ رَحِيمًا ﴿٢٩﴾

STORY 25

THE BORROWED CRAYONS

Layla's crayons had gone missing. She was worried that her teacher, Mrs. Knight, would be mad at her for not having all of her school supplies. *I'll just borrow crayons from Mariam*, she thought. *Nobody has to know.*

When Mariam wasn't looking, Layla reached over and took a purple crayon from Mariam's box. Layla felt bad about being sneaky, but Mariam was her friend. *She would let me borrow them, anyway*, Layla thought.

After a few days, it felt too silly to ask her.

Mrs. Knight asked the children in Room 4 to color the bar chart on their math worksheet. Layla waited patiently until Mariam wasn't looking then snuck a blue crayon from Mariam's box.

A few moments later, Mariam dumped her crayons out. "Have you seen my blue crayon?" she asked.

"Oh, sorry, I must have grabbed yours by accident," Layla said, handing Mariam the blue crayon then pretending to look for her own.

"No worries!" Mariam said.

That was close, Layla thought. *I better ask Mama for new crayons!*

***

As Layla's family sat down for dinner that night, her dad showed them a bill. Dad had been in the hospital, and even with insurance, the family owed a lot of money.

"I really appreciate how you guys have helped the family save money," Dad said. "I know you are giving up a lot, but I'm happy that we can pay these bills now. InshaAllah, things will be back to normal soon." His eyes gleamed with hope. "Bismillah."

"Bismillah," Layla repeated before starting to eat. She was proud of her family for working together through hard times. *I'll just keep sharing crayons with Mariam to save money,* she thought. *It doesn't hurt anything.*

***

The next week, when Layla grabbed half a red crayon from Mariam's box, Mariam caught her red-handed.

"Are you stealing my crayon?" Mariam asked.

"Oh, sorry!" Layla said. "I'm just borrowing it." She handed it back to Mariam. "I didn't think you would mind."

"Maybe not," Mariam said, "but you should *ask* if you want to use my things!"

"I'm sorry. I lost mine," Layla confessed, looking at her hands. "And I don't want to ask my parents for a new box."

"When I got my water bottle from lost and found yesterday, there was a box of crayons in there. Maybe they're yours?"

"Really? Let's go see." Layla raised her hand. "Mrs. Knight, can Mariam and I go look for my crayons in the lost and found?"

"Yes, but hurry back. And if you don't find them, let me know. I always have extra crayons."

The girls hurried off to the lost and found.

Layla opened the crayon box and pulled out the red one. "These can't be mine," she said sadly. "My red crayon is broken."

"Oh, look." Mariam turned the red crayon over. It was marked with Mariam's initials—M.K.

The girls looked at each other and laughed.

Layla said, "If these are *your* crayons, then you must have *mine*!"

"Maybe we should *both* learn to ask before taking someone else's belongings," Mariam said with a laugh. "I'm sorry!"

Layla hugged her friend. "It's okay."

And the girls went back to class, arm-in-arm.

Allah wants us to be honest and not take advantage of what belongs to others. We should make sure we have permission before using someone else's belongings.

BE FORGIVING

(40) The reward of an evil deed is its equivalent. But whoever pardons and seeks reconciliation, then their reward is with Allah. He certainly does not like the wrongdoers.

Ash-Shuraa (The Consultation) 42.40

وَجَزَاءُ سَيِّئَةٍ سَيِّئَةٌ مِّثْلُهَا ۖ فَمَنْ عَفَا وَأَصْلَحَ فَأَجْرُهُ عَلَى اللَّهِ ۚ إِنَّهُ لَا يُحِبُّ الظَّالِمِينَ ﴿٤٠﴾

STORY 26

YASIN'S MODEL AIRPLANE

Samira ran through the house with a model airplane. "*Zoom, zoom, zoom!*" She maneuvered the airplane up and down the long hallway.

"Hey!" Yasin shouted at his sister. "That's not a toy! Give it here."

"Yeah, yeah, you left it in the living room," Samira said, "so I'm playing with it." She spun away from Yasin.

"It's breakable," Yasin said angrily. "Give it to me now!"

Samira turned and shrugged. "Whatever. Here you go." She tossed her brother the airplane.

Yasin reached for the plane but missed. It swooped past his arm and crashed into the wall. *Thud.* It fell to the floor. *Crack!* A wing broke off.

"Oops," Samira said.

"*Oops?*" Yasin stomped his foot. "You broke my airplane!" he shouted. With his hands in fists, he marched past Samira. "You'll pay for this."

He stomped into Samira's room and grabbed a book off her nightstand. "You break my things, I'll teach you." He opened a heavy world records book. *Rip!* He dramatically tore out a page.

"Are you crazy?" Samira shouted. "Stop that! Don't tear any more pages!" She yanked the book from Yasin's hands. *Rip.* Another page tore. "You ... That's it! I'm going to tear up a book of yours."

Samira tossed the world records book on her bed and ran to Yasin's bedroom. He blocked the doorway with his body.

"Let me in," Samira said. She tried to force her way past Yasin.

"No way!" Yasin told her. He grabbed her shoulders and held her back.

After a short struggle, brother and sister stood still, face-to-face. They saw their own emotions—anger, frustration, disappointment, and betrayal—mirrored in the other's eyes.

Samira let out a deep breath. "I didn't mean to break your airplane." She jerked away from her brother's grip.

"I told you not to play with it."

"It was an accident." Samira pointed in his face. "You tore my book on purpose."

Yasin grabbed her arm. "I got my revenge," he said smugly.

"Getting revenge doesn't make me feel any worse about breaking your airplane. It makes me want to get back at you, too."

Yasin thought about that. "You're right." He let go of his sister's arm. "I shouldn't have torn your book," he admitted.

Samira stepped back. They stared at each other.

Yasin remembered something his mother had said: *Forgiveness is better than revenge. Forgive in the way you want to be forgiven.*

He let out a slow breath. "I was very, very angry, but getting back at you didn't help anything. Can you forgive me?"

Samira nodded. "I'm really sorry about your airplane." She picked up the broken pieces from the floor. "Can you forgive me, too?"

"I'm still upset"—Yasin sighed—"but of course I forgive you."

Samira handed the broken pieces to Yasin. "Can it be fixed?"

"Once a part is broken, it never looks as nice." Yasin held the wing to the airplane and studied it. "But I can try. Can you hold it while I glue?"

"Yes," Samira said.

"I'll get out the modeling glue. Afterward, I can tape up your book," Yasin offered.

"Ugh, a taped-up book is the worst!" Samira said with a slight laugh. "We can fix it together, InshaAllah."

Yasin hugged his little sister. "I know it's bad when we fight, but Alhamdulillah we can forgive."

Samira wrapped her arms around him. "Alhamdulillah," she said.

Allah likes it when we forgive others, just like we want Allah and others to forgive us.

LEAD BY EXAMPLE

(44) Do you preach righteousness and fail to practice it yourselves, although you read the Scripture? Do you not understand?

Al-Baqarah (The Cow) 2.44

أَتَأْمُرُونَ النَّاسَ بِالْبِرِّ وَتَنْسَوْنَ أَنْفُسَكُمْ وَأَنْتُمْ تَتْلُونَ الْكِتَابَ ۚ أَفَلَا تَعْقِلُونَ ﴿٤٤﴾

STORY 27

SIGN LANGUAGE CLASS

"It's really important that we *include* everyone," Samira said, smiling. "That's why I want us to learn Sign Language, so we all—boys and girls—can talk to Wendy, and then she feels more included."

Samira had asked Wendy, a deaf student, and Mr. James, her interpreter, to teach them some signs on Wednesdays after school. Besides Samira and Wendy, first graders Hamza, Mariam, Tim, Ali, and Jessica had gathered in the school library for the first Sign Language class.

"Let's start with some signs that we use a lot," Mr. James said, signing as he spoke. "*Yes* and *no*. You try."

The children followed Mr. James, making the signs. They moved their wrists and fingers and repeated, "Yes, no, yes, no."

"Let's try *please* and *thank you*," Mr. James continued. "*Please. Thank you*," he signed.

"This is easy," Mariam said. "*Please. Thank you.*"

Jessica put two signs together. "No, thank you," she said while signing. "This is fun. Let's learn some more!"

"Yes, please," several kids said and signed. Everyone laughed.

Wendy tapped the table excitedly. "You're doing great!" she said, smiling.

"Soon, we'll be talking to you without Mr. James interpreting!" Ali exclaimed. He laughed then checked if Mr. James was offended.

Mr. James grinned and translated for Ali. Then he continued, "Let's work on the alphabet. Then we'll learn how to spell our names. It will take a little practice to learn all the letters, so try each one several times." He started with *A*, and the children practiced with him.

As Mr. James got to the end of the alphabet, a group of kindergarteners in afterschool care came into the library. Mariam's younger cousin, Sara, was in the group and approached the Sign Language class.

"What are you guys doing?" Sara asked.

"Assalam alaykum, Sara. We're learning Sign Language!" Mariam told her as she stood to give Sara a hug.

"Oh, cool!" Sara said. "I want to learn, too!"

"This is just for first graders," Samira said, pointing to the kids at the table. "Not kindergarteners. Sorry."

Mariam leaned close to Samira. "Sara's my cousin. Let's let her join."

Samira shrugged. "We've already started. She's too far behind."

"She can still learn some signs," Tim said.

"The table is already full," Samira argued.

Sara stepped back slowly. "Whatever." She shrugged then slowly went to join her kindergarten group who were browsing the bookshelves.

Ali scooted his chair closer to Jessica, leaving a gap between him and Mariam. "We can make space for her at the table."

Mariam added, "I'll teach her the alphabet this weekend so she's caught up before the next class."

"Let's not forget the whole idea behind this class," Hamza said.

The kids fell silent.

Samira whispered, "To include everyone."

Samira stood and went to Sara. "I'm sorry. I shouldn't have excluded you. Please come join our class."

Sara quickly got a chair and squeezed between Mariam and Ali. "Thank you," she said and signed. Then she signed, "*I'm S-A-R-A, Sara.*"

Wendy gasped. "I'm W-E-N-D-Y, Wendy. You know Sign Language?" she asked.

"*A little,*" Sara signed with a big grin.

Allah wants us to be good. We should always try to be good examples for others. It's important to always do what we say and not just talk about it.

BE PATIENT

(153) O you who believe! Seek help through patience and prayers. Allah is with the patient.

Al-Baqarah (The Cow) 2.153

يَا أَيُّهَا الَّذِينَ آمَنُوا اسْتَعِينُوا بِالصَّبْرِ وَالصَّلَاةِ ۚ إِنَّ اللَّهَ مَعَ الصَّابِرِينَ ﴿١٥٣﴾

STORY 28

IMPATIENT FOR COOKIES

Rami explained his plan for Dad's birthday to his brother Ali. "First, we'll make chocolate chip cookies—that's Dad's favorite!—and when Dad gets home, InshaAllah we'll watch the new superhero movie and eat our cookies!"

In the kitchen, Mom helped the boys set out the ingredients. She handed Rami two sticks of cold butter. "The butter needs to be room temperature," Mom explained. "Set it there by the window, wait until it's soft, then you can mix it with the eggs and sugar." She explained how to read the recipe and what measuring cups to use. "I'm going to lie down for a bit. Let me know if you need help."

Ali and Rami set to work. They cracked eggs and measured sugar.

"Next is the butter," Rami said. "Is it soft yet?"

Ali poked the package. "It's still pretty hard. How long do we have to wait?"

"I don't know," Rami said.

While they waited, they measured the flour, baking soda, and salt then set it aside.

Rami poked the butter. "It's still not soft."

Ali measured out the chocolate chips. Rami lined the cookie sheets with wax paper. Then they checked the butter again.

"This is taking forever. Let's microwave it." Rami put the butter in a bowl and microwaved it for thirty seconds. He poured the melted butter into the sugar mixture, and Ali mixed it up.

"That was way faster than Mom's way," Rami said.

"MashaAllah!" The boys high-fived.

They mixed the ingredients then scooped the mixture onto the cookie sheet.

When the first batch of cookies was in the oven, Rami said, "They look perfect. They'll be done in nine minutes. Let's start the second batch."

While scooping out more cookies, Ali sniffed the air. "They smell yummy! I can't wait for Dad to get home." He peeked in the oven. "Uh-oh, the cookies are running together."

Rami ran over. The dough was spreading out to make one giant connected cookie. He went to get his mom.

Mom knew right away. "This happens when the butter is melted rather than at room temperature."

"Oops," Rami said. "We should have been more patient."

The timer went off, and he carefully took the flat cookies out of the oven.

"They're totally ruined!"

"These cookies will taste okay," Mom said, "but they'll be crispy, not soft."

"Dad will be so disappointed!" Ali said.

"Maybe we can make a big cookie cake?" Rami suggested.

"A crunchy cookie cake will be hard to eat," Mom said.

"We should start over," Ali said.

Rami tapped his chin, thinking. "What if we make a cookie cake and then crumble it to make an ice cream topping?"

"That sounds delicious," Mom said.

Rami and Ali rolled out the dough into a giant cookie. When it was done baking, the boys walked to the corner store to buy ice cream.

Before too long, Dad came home from work and called to the boys, "Movie time! Cookie time!"

"We aren't having cookies," Rami said, hanging his head.

"What? You promised me birthday cookies!" Dad said with a laugh. "And the house smells like cookies!"

"We weren't patient enough to make them correctly," Rami confessed.

Ali hugged his dad. "We want to turn the messed-up cookies into cookie-crumble ice cream sundaes. How does that sound?"

"That sounds like a good change of plans," Dad said.

Rami and Ali served up sundaes, and they all sat down to enjoy the movie.

"Happy birthday, Dad," Rami and Ali said.

Good things happen when you are patient and do what's right. Just believe in Allah's plan and be patient, and you'll see how good things will come to you.

BE KIND

(28) But if you must turn them down 'because you lack the means to give'—while hoping to receive your Lord's bounty— then 'at least' give them a kind word.

Al-Israa (The Night Journey) 17.28

وَإِمَّا تُعْرِضَنَّ عَنْهُمُ ابْتِغَاءَ رَحْمَةٍ مِنْ رَبِّكَ تَرْجُوهَا فَقُلْ لَهُمْ قَوْلًا مَيْسُورًا ﴿٢٨﴾

STORY 29

FATIMA'S BROKEN LEG

Mrs. Henderson had already taken Monday's attendance and had started teaching when Fatima peeked her head in the door. Her teacher paused the lesson.

"Good morning, Fatima."

Fatima strained. "Can someone help me with the door?"

Tim jumped up and held the door open for Fatima.

Everyone saw why Fatima needed help. She had a cast on her right leg and crutches under her arms.

"Oh dear, what happened to you?" Mrs. Henderson asked.

"I fell off the trampoline and broke my leg," Fatima answered. She looked up at her teacher. "I'm sorry I'm late. I'm still learning to get around on these crutches."

"Do you need help?" Malak asked.

Samira jumped up and offered, "Let me help you with your books."

She took Fatima's backpack and set it next to her desk. Tim pulled out Fatima's chair to help her sit. Fatima held Samira's hand as she swiveled on one leg into her seat. Lily grabbed the crutches and laid them neatly on the other side of Fatima's chair.

"Thanks, guys!" Fatima said, sitting at her desk.

Malak stood by awkwardly. "I'm sorry. I wanted to help, but everyone was quicker than me.

Do you need anything else?"

Fatima sighed. "No, thanks. I'm good now."

"Oh," Malak said. "Okay." She frowned.

Mrs. Henderson continued her lesson. When it was time for group work, Tim and Wendy moved their desks so Fatima could stay in her seat. Samira made sure no one bumped Fatima's leg. Jessica brought Fatima her art box from the shelf.

"Alhamdulillah, everyone is being so kind," Fatima said.

"Is there something I can do?" Malak asked, hopeful.

"I think we got it," Jessica said, handing Fatima her art box.

After work time, Mrs. Henderson sent the class out to recess.

"Let me help you up," Jessica said, offering Fatima a hand.

"I'll push in your chair," Ali offered.

Lily carefully handed Fatima her crutches. "Ready?"

"Yes, thank you," Fatima said as she stepped toward the door.

Malak crossed the room to Fatima. "Can I help?" she asked. She looked for something she could move or carry for Fatima.

"No, thanks. I've got it now," Fatima told her.

Hamza held the door for the girls then went to join his friends.

Malak walked slowly. "I feel like a bad friend. Everyone was helping you, but I didn't get a chance to do a kind deed."

"I'm a little embarrassed that everyone is making such a fuss," Fatima admitted as she watched her friends run outside ahead of her. She carefully took another slow step. "It looks like I'll be the last one to recess for the next few weeks."

Malak nodded and started to hurry outside, but then she paused. "Can I walk with you?"

Fatima smiled at Malak. "That would be the kindest thing anyone has done all day."

Malak tilted her head. "So, how *did* you fall off the trampoline?"

"Well," Fatima started, "it's a funny story ..."

Talking and laughing, they slowly walked to recess together.

Allah wants us to be kind to everyone, especially those who need it. Even if we can't give them anything, we should still say nice words and do kind deeds to make them feel better.

THINK CRITICALLY AND ACT WITH CLARITY

(83) When some news of security or alarm comes their way, they broadcast it. But had they referred it to the Messenger, and to those in authority among them, those who can draw conclusions from it would have comprehended it (...)

An-Nisa (The Women) 4.83 Revealed in Madinah

وَإِذَا جَاءَهُمْ أَمْرٌ مِنَ الْأَمْنِ أَوِ الْخَوْفِ أَذَاعُوا بِهِ ۖ وَلَوْ رَدُّوهُ إِلَى الرَّسُولِ وَإِلَى أُولِي الْأَمْرِ مِنْهُمْ لَعَلِمَهُ الَّذِينَ يَسْتَنْبِطُونَهُ مِنْهُمْ (...) ﴿٨٣﴾

STORY 30

EID AL-FITR SURPRISE

On the last day of Ramadan, the children were volunteering at the mosque, organizing boxes of food for needy families.

"I can't wait to celebrate Eid al-Fitr tomorrow!" Omar told his friends.

Mariam put a jar of jam in each food box. "I'm very excited about the big gift!" she said.

"Me, too," Ali proclaimed, packing cans of corn in the boxes. "It's supposed to be really cool."

"You're getting a big gift for Eid al-Fitr?" Layla asked.

"Didn't you hear?" Mariam said. "Malak's aunt Khadija bought something special for everyone who helped at the mosque this week."

Layla stopped working. "I'm pretty sure it's a doll! I'm going to buy a whole set of new doll dresses after we finish packing."

"It's not a doll," Omar told her with his hands on his hips. "I bet it's a skateboard. Ms. Khadija heard me talking about how much I wanted to try the new skatepark! I'll invite my friend to try it with me."

"I think we're wasting our time guessing," Layla said, noticing that everyone had stopped working. "We're supposed to be helping needy families today."

Mariam shrugged. "We don't even know if this is true. Fatima said she overheard Malak say that her aunt asked her for gifts ideas for us."

Layla nodded. "It's important to make sure information is correct before sharing it with others. What if it was only a question? Or what if Ms. Khadija changed her mind?"

Ali laughed. "Looks like the 'big gift' is just a rumor! It's always best to make sure something is true before making plans around it, don't you think?"

"Great thinking, Ali! To know if it's true, we should find out where the rumor came from. That way, we can be sure it's correct," Mariam said with a big smile.

"Wait! What? Are you just going to ask Ms. Khadija?" Omar questioned.

"He-he. Nope, not me," Mariam whispered. "I'll ask my mom to call and discreetly ask her."

Everyone laughed. "Now, let's get back to work."

Everyone went back to packing food in boxes, and just in time for pickup. They had forty-eight boxes ready to deliver. Everyone loaded the boxes into Omar's mom's car.

"Let's go!" Omar said. "Time to deliver to the Community Food Pantry!"

"Let's wait," Omar's mom said softly. "Ms. Khadija is coming with a surprise for you guys."

Everyone froze, wide-eyed and smiling.

Layla whispered, "It's true."

Ali burst out, "What is it? What's the surprise?"

Omar's mom grinned. "I can't tell you because *it's a surprise*!"

Everyone laughed.

"Sounds like you're having fun," a newcomer said.

Everyone turned. "Ms. Khadija!" they shouted together.

She hugged all the boys and girls then pulled a stack of notecards from her purse. "I have something for you, to thank you for being goodhearted Muslims and to celebrate Eid al-Fitr."

Everyone was silent, excited to finally see what the big gift was!

Anyone could see the joy and excitement on everyone's face as they received the notecards, which contained the following message:

> *I'm very excited to inform you that we'll be spending the second day of El-Eid together. We're going to have a wild adventure at the Safari Park! After that, we'll have a yummy lunch together. And to finish the day, we'll go for some fast-paced fun at the go-kart track! Meet me here at 9:30 and let's have a blast!*

The children cheered, hugged, and high-fived.

"This is the best gift ever!" Mariam cheered. "Thank you very much."

"Yes, thank you so much," Layla added. "It's going to be really fun!"

"We would never have guessed this!" Ali said with a big smile.

Omar nodded gratefully. "Alhamdulillah, we are blessed!"

Always check the facts before sharing information. Ask those in authority or the messenger for clarification to make sure you understand it correctly. That way, you will avoid spreading false information and make wise decisions.

Made in the USA
Las Vegas, NV
07 November 2024

11252483R00072